Witness in His Own Cause

Gustav Just

Witness in His Own Cause

The Fifties in the German Democratic Republic

Translated from the German
by
Oliver Lu

Foreword by
Christoph Hein
and
Introduction by
Henry Krisch

University Press of America, Inc.
Lanham • New York • London

Copyright © 1995 by
University Press of America,® Inc.
4720 Boston Way
Lanham, Maryland 20706

3 Henrietta Street
London, WC2E 8LU England

Library of Congress Cataloging-in-Publication Data

Just, Gustav.
(Zeuge in eigener Sache. English)
Witness in his own cause : the Fifties in the German Democratic
Republic / Gustav Just ; with a foreword by Christoph Hein; translated
from the German by Oliver Lu ; introduction by Henry Krisch.
p.   cm.
Translation of: Zeuge in eigener Sache.
Includes index.
1. Just, Gustav. 2. Political prisoners--Germany (East)--Biography.
3. Germany (East)--Politics and government. I. Title.
HV9680.5.J87A3   1995   365'.45'092 --dc20   95-33441 CIP
(B)

ISBN 0-7618-0107-3 (cloth: alk: ppr.)

⊖™The paper used in this publication meets the minimum
requirements of American National Standard for Information
Sciences—Permanence of Paper for Printed Library Materials,
ANSI Z39.48—1984

Contents

" . . . and others"
(for Gustav Just)

Only a few months ago I offered Gustav Just a place of refuge: a copy of his memoirs was to be left in my apartment, along with the manuscripts and documents of other friends who likewise had reason to fear that a third party might be after their papers. I could offer at best a precarious refuge. Its safety consisted solely in the hoped-for ignorance of the dreaded third party, for I could hardly have fended off a real attempt at snatching these materials.

That was a few months ago, and yet it seems so long ago. Times change. To be sure, they do not change on their own. And they might change again if we do not remain vigilant. People's freedom can be won only in a battle, in a revolution or a reformation. Freedom is never lost all at once, though. Freedom does not end unexpectedly or with a bang, freedom dies one inch at a time. And every one of us carries the responsibility for losing even one inch.

Gustav Just appears here as a witness in his own cause, but also as a witness to his times and the history of this country. His book will alter our writing of that history. What Just describes here was up to now described in three short, pithy sentences produced by a collective of politicians and historians—for which they were highly decorated—that were supposed to be valid for all time:

> In Berlin and other cities counterrevolutionary groups began forming. They were composed mainly of intellectuals isolated from the people, and proposed programs for the elimination of the workers' and peasants' power. Before they could threaten the peace and jeopardize the socialist achievements of the people, the security organs of the Republic stopped them in their tracks. (*History of the German Workers' Movement*, Volume 8, Berlin 1966)

Just's book destroys a mendacious and cynical view of the world to which so many people contributed, people who already knew the truth but were not willing to stand up for it. Also contributing and sharing the guilt were those who did not muster the courage— and much courage was surely needed—to free the truth from the stranglehold of a corrupt power. Just's book helps us dismantle a world-view that many, that all of us accepted, more or less knowing that it was mendacious, that it was directed against us because it sought to control us. It aimed to kill our memory and recollections in order to win over our souls.

Just's book will give us back a piece of our memories. We will thereby recover a piece of our own dignity, for which we should stand up more bravely in the future.

And perhaps his book will help us save something of the dream, of our hopes for a social order more worthy of human beings, that hope which in the fate of people like Just was so grievously insulted and injured, and almost destroyed.

The legal proceedings against Just were conducted under the heading of "Janka and others." Even the recently introduced measures towards his rehabilitation fall under the same generalizing concept. That is not merely a bureaucratic necessity. The limited capacity of our memory, our imperfect ability to remember, always makes the abbreviated form " . . . and others" necessary when it is a question not only of an individual, but of several, of many, of very many people.

With individual crimes we can come to grips: perpetrators and victims have a name and a face. But when a crime is multiplied, when it becomes incalculable in extent as it widens in scope, it becomes practically anonymous.

The victims of Stalinism in the Soviet Union can be grasped only by means of huge and for us largely abstract numbers; they have become nameless because our imagination fails in the face of the no longer graspable multitude of victims; our eyes, our ears, our memory are incapable of grasping mass murder and wholesale crime.

The formulation " . . . and others" is a product of our frailty.

With this phrase the authorities and the state's attorney imply that they will forget no one, but will subject everyone to the prevailing justice—or the prevailing injustice.

With that same phrase we say that we do not want to forget any of the victims. But precisely this " . . . and others" is, and we know it, the first step toward forgetting. The phrase is supposed to encompass something that simultaneously vanishes behind it. It is supposed to reassure us, inform us that our memory is wide awake, but in its abstractness the names and the faces have already been erased.

One of them, Gustav Just, has stepped forward to give us a report, to testify as a witness to the past. Yet what he has to say to us is not just information about the past and the state in which we lived, and still live. We will hear something about our years and decades of silence, about our courage and our cowardice, about our ability to live with each other in a humanistic, socialist, Christian way or to submit to the pressure of intolerance and the little daily betrayals. We will hear something about ordinary socialism in our country, about a society that was already calling itself socialist. We will learn something about ourselves.

For Gustav Just and the others were our neighbors in those years. We knew them, and we were aware, more or less, of the injustice inflicted upon them. The witness in his own cause who now steps forward is also a witness against us, he testifies to our helplessness. We will have to listen to this witness's testimony with horror and with shame. For our own sake we should use his evidence for the future, so that in the future we muster more courage and strength, more backbone, and never again allow such a deformation of society, never again allow ourselves to become deformed.

There were innumerable victims of Stalinism in the countries of Stalinism. The terror ranged from murder and judicial murder to minor, everyday harassment. In recent years it was not the hangman that threatened, but rather prison or a closed psychiatric ward or expatriation. But in recent years there were also other changes: along with the easing of terror came growing, spreading solidarity, and protest against terror. And it was with this changed outlook that the new, the later victims saw their almost omnipotent oppressors.

I believe that all those who in recent years were thrown into prison, who were forced to leave their country or subjected to repression, that these later victims no longer saw in the people sitting across the table from them their friend or comrade or fellow-combatant, no longer the upright Communist or the valiant humanist; the later victims saw in their torturers only the all-powerful and cynical representatives of a merciless machine. And I believe that this knowledge, this other outlook alleviated somewhat their terrible fate.

For many of Stalinism's earlier victims, from Bukharin in the Soviet Union to the victims in our country, Gustav Just and Walter Janka and Heinz Zöger and Richard Wolf and Erich Loest and Ralf Schröder and Jochen Wenzel and others, these occurrences—apart from the unspeakable nature and brutality of the terror—were especially insulting and degrading and incomprehensible because these men were and had to be convinced that those who were condemning them actually stood shoulder to shoulder with them, that everything was a misunderstanding which their old fellow-combatants and comrades would soon clear up. Because of this inability to understand, the terror, the verdict, and the sentence were especially horrible for them. All the documents and their own notes attest to this.

The revelations in the Soviet Union and in recent weeks and days in our country contribute, I believe, to their rehabilitation. Now it is evident to them and to everyone: their self-appointed judges were the enemies of the people, the saboteurs of the economy, crooks and profiteers, members of a mafia whose goal was the destruction of socialism. Everything with which they charged their victims, the victims of Stalinism, and for which they condemned innocent people, applied to them.

Toward the end of the seventies the Stalinist purges in the GDR caused a major convulsion in the state, a convulsion whose after-shocks became one of the causes of the changes now occurring. Many people no longer accepted in silence the expatriation and expulsion of intellectuals and artists who refused to be disciplined.

Yet for Gustav Just and many others there was no help. He had to serve his sentence, two years of it in solitary confinement. When he now, as one of the hitherto nameless victims, testifies publicly, we should not forget that other victims of Stalinism in our country remain unknown because they can no longer step forward, because not everyone has that possibility and also because it exceeds our physical and mental stamina to hear all the witnesses. We should not forget: the number of other victims is almost infinite. And it is not only writers, artists, doctors, and other intellectuals. It was likewise craftsman and tradesman, and—last but not least and despite the so-called workers' and peasants' state—workers and peasants. Many of these victims are no longer our fellow countrymen. They have left our country because they wanted to leave or were forced to, because they were driven out by the oppressive machinery of ordinary Stalinism.

Anyone who still tries today to tell you that he knows and knew nothing about it must be very young or must have been blind and dumb all his life.

I hope that Gustav Just as witness will contribute to our mustering the strength and the courage to renew, in spite of everything, our society's foundations and abolish the so-called existing socialism, which was nothing more than a system in which a small political clique, through an all-powerful secret police and an almost seamless web of surveillance and denunciation, spying and repression, held in check and exploited an entire people.

I hope that his testimony will help us muster the courage and strength not to capitulate in spite of everything, but to establish for the first time on German soil a society that does justice to humanistic ideals, Christian as well as socialist.

In all these years we had reason and cause enough to despair, but we held on. And more than that: the people have raised themselves to an upright gait. Now a morass of unimagined proportions is coming to light. Today, as we start to explore the morass of corruption, of abuse of office, of the existing Stalinism in the GDR—and we are just starting, because this morass extends over our whole country—we are seized with horror.

We have reason to hope, however. A morass is dangerous and deadly as long as it is unfamiliar. It is terrifying when one first encounters it. Yet as soon as we begin to drain it, it loses much of its horror. We should welcome these terrible and terrifying disclosures, should look forward to them almost cheerfully.

The revelations will make the recently introduced reform irreversible. And they are necessary not only for the sake of justice. We need them for our future. And on the horizon, where the end of the morass can be glimpsed, something very precious glimmers: a more humane society. For the first time a word crosses my lips that I have hitherto been unable to pronounce. For the first time in more than forty years I can say: This country here will be my country. It will be my country if I do not give up on it!

Let us not despair! For four decades there was sufficient reason to despair. Let us not lose hope in the face of the morass! Let us not give up! That this morass has come into view is a sign of our success. At last we have a chance. Only now do we have it. And we should—because we finally won it through struggle—use it for ourselves and not let it slip away.

After thirteen years of fascism and forty years of Stalinism this chance is very slim. But it is at hand. It is only now at hand. We should plant our seedlings this very day.

4 December 1989
CHRISTOPH HEIN

Introduction

by Henry Krisch

In this book, Gustav Just bears witness to a crucial part of his life and career, and to the ideas that were important to him during the years between 1953 and 1958, in 1962, and during the period when he was compiling the book (1989). What will the English-language reader find in Oliver Lu's excellent translation of Just's testimony?

For the interested general reader, as well as for the scholar, Gustav Just's *Witness in His Own Cause* vividly illuminates a central intellectual, moral, and political drama of our times. This drama focuses on the often uneasy relationship between culture and power. In this book Just captures the hopes and illusions of socially committed intellectuals, describes how those hopes were disappointed and the illusions shattered, and reveals how cruelly the state responded to criticism intended to be constructive.

This drama also has a human dimension. We see character destroyed by fear and ambition, and social commitment soured into bitter cynicism; yet we also see women and men seeking to live lives of honor and meaning. Such a goal, in this fearsome century, particularly in Europe, and especially in Germany seems almost more than human effort and character can achieve. So we see great effort rewarded by political failure, repaid by brutality, and justice—when it comes at all—much delayed and never complete.

To those interested in German history or Communist politics, this book offers an instructive case history. Here a key participant shows how the Communist regime in East Germany used, manipulated, feared, rewarded, and punished writers and editors. The leaders of the German Democratic Republic (GDR), like those of other Communist countries, paid intellectuals such as Gustav Just the sincere but frightening compliment of taking him seriously as a threat. In 1957, Gustav Just was tried, convicted and sentenced to prison, charged with plotting the overthrow of the state and its social order.[1]

The East German ruling party, the SED, viewed Communist (or closely fellow-traveling) intellectuals as an important resource for administering and advertising the "actually existing socialism" of the GDR. However the rulers never felt confident that the intellectuals were as steadfast as non-intellectual party bureaucrats. The intellectuals' works were "achievements" to be heralded—but might not those works be a subversively combustible mixture, threatening to undermine the regime? Since power in Communist countries was ultimately justified by an intellectual argument, these regimes could not but take words (and images) seriously.

As a result, GDR politics were regularly punctuated by hostile confrontations between regime and intellectuals.[2] As the novelist Christoph Hein points out in his foreword, until the 1980s, most dissenting intellectuals assumed that they shared objectives with those in power; thus the criminalization of their efforts at constructive reform and subsequent incarceration by "their" government were especially hurtful.

Gustav Just—self-described as a "Socialist Youth, soldier and officer under Hitler's banner, *Neulehrer** in the Soviet zone, member for six years in the SED Party apparatus, secretary-general of the German Writers' Union for a year, editor of *Sonntag*"—was born in a German-speaking community in Bohemia in 1921. Like many East German Communists, he came from an ostensibly internationalist Marxist movement—his father had been a founder of the Communist Party of Czechoslovakia. While that connection did not prevent the Justs' expulsion from Czechoslovakia in 1946, Gustav Just remained closely linked to intellectual circles in both Prague and Warsaw. The fact that these ties aroused the suspicion of the Ulbricht regime highlights the extent to which the SED leaders feared and scorned efforts at political and intellectual reform in the "fraternal" East European parties and countries.

As a nineteen-year old, Just had volunteered for military service in Hitler's army. In the Ukraine in July 1941, the young enlisted man's unit was asked by Ukrainian peasants to defend their village from marauders whom they described as "Jewish terrorists." This involved Just in the execution of six of these "terrorists."[3]

The entire affair is marked by the irony symptomatic of this period in East German history, when one considers the actions and motivations of all concerned. Just's diary contains the only evidence of this episode. The diary entry shows the nineteen-year old soldier wondered whether shooting the suspects was justified even if the six victims had in fact been thieves.

---

*Literally "new-teacher," refers to instructors in the Soviet zone of occupation who were hurriedly trained in 8-month courses to replace teachers suspected of affiliation with the Nazi Party.—Tr.

The diary was seized by Stasi agents who searched Just's home after his arrest, which had occurred while he was in court testifying in the related trial of Wolfgang Harich! The East German authorities thus knew of this incident from 1957 on, but chose not to reveal it. Either they hoped later to blackmail Just later on, or, more likely, they hoped to avoid the embarrassing revelation that Just had held responsible positions in the GDR despite his past. Nonetheless, regime loyalists used the affair to discredit Just among fellow GDR intellectuals by hinting that underneath his socialist exterior, Just was just a "regular anti-Semite."

Gustav Just himself seems to have repressed this episode,[4] but its exposure after the fall of the Wall ended his second effort to work in East Germany for social democratic reforms. Although he had joined the opposition that toppled the Honecker regime, the public disgrace showered on him after the wartime incident came to light in March 1992 led Just to resign as an SPD member of the Brandenburg state legislature.

The central events described in this book took place in 1956-57, when Just and other reform-minded East German intellectuals tried to use Khrushchev's revelations of Stalin's crimes as a lever to bring reform to the GDR. They thought that revulsion against Stalinism would turn their fellow citizens (and especially fellow party members) against the Ulbricht leadership; a renewed party would then lead to a more open society in the GDR, as well as closer to German unification.

Both Just's diary entries and his published writings from that era make clear that the intellectuals always intended their reforms to remain well within the ambit of the system. For Gustav Just in 1956, democratization meant "promoting the creative participation of all segments of the population in building socialism, that is, to make the issue of socialism an issue for every individual citizen . . . " (p. 105). Although Just approved of the 1956 reform efforts in both Poland and Hungary, he later decided the Nagy regime in Hungary had gone too far, and that military intervention had been justified (pp. 75–76).

But as would be true throughout the history of the GDR—and indeed, in the post-Stalin USSR as well—this sort of loyal opposition proved unwelcome to the regime. In 1962 Gustav Just still hoped that "right, morality, and decency" (p. 90) would triumph in the party; instead, later under Honecker as earlier under Ulbricht, the party responded by closing ranks, whether out of fear or conviction, against the reformers, who paid for their efforts with jail sentences, professional and political demotion, or exile to the West.

Inasmuch as Ulbricht was almost overthrown both in 1953 and 1956 (his removal in 1971 had comparatively less to do with domestic issues), Just's hopes were not completely without foundation. Just must have known the dangers of defying the regime, not as an intriguer within the leadership, but as an open critic; his protestations that neither he nor his colleagues wanted to overthrow Ulbricht raises the obvious question: why not? It seems that their stance may have resulted from a realistic sense of the danger of challenging the regime directly. In one particularly poignant diary passage, Just notes: "I am not in agreement with [Ulbricht's policies] and am convinced that many [others] think the same. . . . I will be very careful not to say that out loud." (p. 4)[5]

From the SED leadership's perspective, the problem was to contain the forces of change unleashed by the revelations about Stalin. Ulbricht had sought to preempt calls for change by declaring that Stalin's works had never been counted as a classic of Marxism-Leninism, and that there had been no personality cult in the GDR. In fact (as Gustav Just's diary entries reveal), the struggle for reform in the GDR had been underway since 1953. At each crisis, proponents of reform within the leadership, allied with reform-minded intellectuals, had tried to remove the Ulbricht group and steer the GDR toward reform. Each time a combination of domestic politics, personalities, and the external Cold War setting had combined to rescue the hard-line faction.[6]

Indeed, while Gustav Just's struggles formed his own personal drama, they also exemplified a political relationship characteristic of the GDR. As has been suggested, the relationship between the political leadership and critical yet loyal intellectuals was always strained and uneasy. For example, the years immediately following the building of the Berlin Wall saw a cultural thaw, especially in film, that corresponded to the official loosening of economic controls (the so-called NÖSPL). But this greater freedom was soon followed by renewed repression. All the themes of Just's struggles, as well as concerns over "Western cultural pessimism" and "decadent" youth culture, were on the agenda of the notorious 11th Plenum of the SED Central Committee in December 1965.[7]

The crackdown of 1965 was followed by Honecker's widely-noted remark, made upon his accession to the party leadership in 1971, that in literature and the arts there should be "no taboos" for anyone working from a socialist perspective. This ostensible liberalization did not preclude the regime's expatriation of the balladeer Wolf Biermann in 1979, despite the massive and semi-public protests that followed. Even in the regime's latter days in 1988, the authorities exiled some writers and antagonized others by banning Soviet publications that contained too much *perestroika*.

This cycle of reform and repression continued even in the tumultuous days of 1989. In May 1989, the GDR bestowed the "Service to the Fatherland" medal in gold to Walter Janka—without mentioning his previous arrest and conviction. In October, Janka gave a reading from his memoirs in a Berlin theater. On November 4, prominent writers such as Christa Wolf and Stefan Heym took part in the great demonstration on Berlin's Alexanderplatz.

In January 1990, the GDR Supreme Court voided the 1957 convictions and sentences of Just, Janka, and two fellow defendants, Richard Wolf and Heinz Zöger. The political power that had first persecuted and then ignored them had collapsed; the state that had convicted them only now to reverse its verdict had only ten months to live. The socialist cause, for which Just and others had striven and suffered, was undergoing an enormous political defeat. But the idealism, the devotion to the public good, and the conviction that the arts can work to liberate humanity—the qualities to which Gustav Just bears witness in this book—will remain, and his record of them will continue to do him honor.

---

[1] Just was arrested in March 1957, sentenced to a four-year jail term in July 1957, and freed in a general amnesty in November 1960. For an account of these events by a fellow defendant—and of course much else besides—see Walter Janka, *Schwierigkeiten mit der Wahrheit* (Reinbeck bei Hamburg: Rowohlt, 1989).

[2] For a general account of these relations, see David Pike, *The Politics of Culture in Soviet-Occupied Germany* (Stanford: Stanford University Press, 1992).

[3] Just's own retrospective account can be found in an interview he gave in November 1990 to the editors of a book on the Kulturbund: Magdalena Heider & Kerstin Thöns, ed., *SED und Intellektuelle in der DDR der fünfziger Jahre. Kulturbund-Protokolle* (Bonn: Edition Deutschland Archiv, 1990), p. 153, n. 14. See also, Hanno Kuhnert's thoughtful and balanced account, "Die Schüsse im Leben des Gustav Just," *Die Zeit* 4/16/1993.

---

[4]The parallels to contemporary revelations about the Stasi connections of a Christa Wolf or Heiner Müller, or of the Polish intelligence connections of Marcel Reich-Ranicki, suggest that intellectuals may be persuaded to undertake dubious political acts, but remain uneasy about thus supping with the devil.

[5]Both Just and Janka, in their memoirs, cast a pitiless light on the moral collapse of those famous writers who failed to intercede for them in public while encouraging them in private; this applies especially to Johannes Becher and Anna Seghers. What is the appropriate answer to Becher's retort to Just—whether he (Just) thought it had been easy for Becher "to sit night after night in the Hotel Lux [in Moscow in the 1930s] with his bags packed"?

[6]The SED subsequently dropped the accusation that intellectuals such as Just had sought to overthrow the regime. In an official account prepared by the SED's Academy of Social Sciences, the authors declare that for "not a few citizens of the GDR ... especially among intellectuals ... " the process of seeing events from the correct ideological perspective "was a lengthy and difficult one." *Die SED und das kulturelle Erbe* (Berlin: Dietz, 1988), p. 224.

[7]Günter Agde, ed., *Kahlschlag. Das 11. Plenum des ZK der SED 1965. Studien und Dokumente.* (Berlin: Aufbau, 1991). Just prior to this meeting, a group of writers was exhorted by a party official, Marianne Lange, to produce " ... literature that leads us to a productive relationship with society." Cited in Günter Agde, "Zur Anatomie eines Tests. Das Gespräch Walter Ulbrichts mit Schriftstellern und Künstlern am 25. November 1965 im Staatsrat der DDR," ibid., pp. 128-47. Agde points out (p. 130) that, while planning this "conversation," party leaders never asked artists and writers what questions they might have for the leadership!

Abbreviations

BZ *Berliner Zeitung* (daily newspaper in East Berlin)

CC Central Committee of the SED (*q.v.*)

Com. Comrade

CPSU Communist Party of the Soviet Union

DEFA *Deutsche Film Aktiengesellschaft* (East) German Film Company

DFD *Demokratischer Frauenbund Deutschlands* Democratic Women's League of Germany

DSV *Deutscher Schriftstellerverband* German Writers' Union

FDGB *Freier Deutscher Gewerkschaftsbund* Free German Trade Union Federation

FDJ *Freie Deutsche Jugend* Free German Youth

GDR German Democratic Republic (East Germany)

Gestapo *Geheime Staatspolizei* Secret State Police (under Nazi regime 1933–45)

HO *Handelsorganisation* Trading Organization (state retailing body)

KPD *Kommunistische Partei Deutschlands* Communist Party of Germany

KPÖ *Kommunistische Partei Österreichs* Communist Party of Austria

KuBa penname of Kurt Barthel (1914–67), secretary-general of the German Writers' Union (1952–54), Central Committee member (1954–67).

LPG *Landwirtschaftliche Produktionsgenossenschaft* Agricultural Producers Cooperative

MTS *Maschinen-Traktorenstation* Machinery and Tractor Station

NKVD [Soviet] People's Commissariat for Internal Affairs (Soviet
secret police during World War Two)

RIAS *Rundfunk im amerikanischen Sektor* Radio in the American
Sector

SED *Sozialistische Einheitspartei Deutschlands* Socialist Unity
Party of Germany

SMA(D) *Sowjetische Militäradministration (in Deutschland)*
Soviet Military Adminstration (in Germany)

SPD *Sozialdemokratische Partei Deutschlands* Social Democratic
Party of Germany

Stasi *Staatssicherheitsdienst* State Security Service (East Germany)

SU *Sowjetunion* Soviet Union

I

The New Course—The 17th of June—The 20th Party Congress

(Diaries 1957/1989)

July 1989 *The world has begun to move. A specter is haunting Europe, but not the specter of Communism, as Marx declared in the middle of the last century, but the specter of the irresistible urge for freedom of those peoples in whose countries freedoms have been curtailed.*

More and more, Gorbachev is becoming the focus of hopes. It is not only in the truly socialist countries that phrases such as perestroika, glasnost, *and "new thinking" are making their rounds— to the leaders of some of these countries they probably seem more like demons. A few of these socialist countries are making an attempt to reform their systems so that their populations will feel more comfortable, materially and spiritually. Yes, the world has begun to move.*

One's thoughts go back to the Fifties, when after the Twentieth Party Congress of the Soviet Communist Party a similar movement began to manifest itself, likewise giving rise to great hopes. At that time, in February 1957, I began to keep a diary, to which I gave the title "At the Turning-Point." That I interpreted the period that way bears witness to my naiveté and my illusions, which shortly thereafter were destroyed in a new Ice Age, and which landed me for four years in a prison run by that state to whose reconstruction I had committed all my energy for a good decade. The diary was written in a hurry, with a rash pen. Many of my formulations are contestable, but retaining the authenticity of my thinking at the time is more important to me than balance and style. I am therefore keeping the text as it was, with insertions where I feel them to be necessary from a contemporary perspective.

13 February 1957 To begin something on the thirteenth, even a diary like this—a little voice inside one protests, a remnant of the superstitious Middle Ages that lives on in us all. Yet perhaps this same 13th will bring luck in this topsy-turvy world! If the world is already standing on its head, why shouldn't a black cat crossing one's path augur luck and a chimney-sweep misfortune? The world is standing on its head? Perhaps not, when in the German Democratic Republic—that section of Germany freed by the Red Army and ruled by the SED, a victorious coalition of Communists and Social Democrats—Communists and Social Democrats are thrown into prison?

Sitting in prison right now, though not yet convicted, is Walter Janka, director of the Aufbau-Verlag, a young communist from Chemnitz, an emigrant, a Spanish Civil War veteran, the type of Communist who became a hero in the partisans' resistance: unyielding, loyal, a revolutionary to the bone. He is sitting in a Stasi prison in connection with the arrest of another Communist, Dr. Wolfgang Harich. Harich is the best philosopher we have, still young, came over to us from the bourgeoisie. He is supposedly the head of a counterrevolutionary conspiracy, which, if one believes Ulbricht, had as its goal nothing less than the overthrow of the peoples' democracy in the GDR. The organizational center of this group was allegedly, as Ulbricht reported at the 30th Plenum of the Central Committee, the Aufbau-Verlag and *Sonntag*, and that's where I come in. Until three weeks ago, you see, I was acting editor in chief of that newspaper, and, as everybody knows, was friends with Janka and Harich. Because I would presumably be aware of this plot, but am not, it seems to me that Ulbricht is lying. That is why I decided to write this diary. Whether it will ever be read by eyes other than mine is impossible to know. Possibly Ulbricht and his people will remain in power. Then they'll write the history of the Party, which will look like this: "In the year 1956 the correction of several errors was initiated by the Twentieth Party Congress of the Soviet Communist Party. This was used by reactionaries as a pretext to launch a fierce attack on the unity of the Party and the socialist camp. In Hungary they succeeded in unleashing a counterrevolutionary uprising. Also in the GDR a group of intellectuals who had succumbed to bourgeois ideology (Harich, Janka, Just, and others), tried to undermine the foundations of the power of the workers and peasants. Through the vigilance of the Party and Com. Ulbricht these counterrevolutionary worms were ground underfoot, and the people went back to the order of the day."

July 1989 *That last sentence was inspired by the wording used by the authoritative* History of the Soviet Communist Party *to describe the liquidation of all the Bolsheviks who had fallen out of favor. Our Stalinists had become a bit more clever, and so the corresponding passage in the* History of the Workers' Movement *reads: "In Berlin and other cities counterrevolutionary groups began forming. They were composed mainly of intellectuals isolated from the people, and proposed programs for the elimination of the workers' and peasants' power. Before they could threaten the peace and jeopardize the socialist achievements of the people, the security organs of the Republic stopped them in their tracks."*

Because the head of the team of authors was Walter Ulbricht himself, one should not be surprised at this sort of "historiography."

13 February 1957 They would write something more or less like that. Because the situation was entirely different and—as long as there's an ounce of sense to history—will turn out differently, I must write down how I experienced this period and what I know about it. If we fail politically, at least my children will know what the truth was. If we succeed, however,—who this "we" is will be apparent from what follows—then the time will come when these notes can be published.

July 1989 Even now the time has not come, although a beginning has been made by Gorbachev. In the Soviet Union all of Stalin's victims have been rehabilitated, and in Hungary the victims of the terror that followed the suppression of the people's uprising in 1956. With hundreds of thousands looking on, Imre Nagy was taken out of an anonymous massgrave and moved to a more worthy resting place. Only in the GDR has silence continued to reign over the misdeeds of a Party leadership that has held power continuously since 1945 and is still not ready to practice self-criticism. It will not, however, be able to swim against the stream in the long run. Out of this conviction I have taken out my old diary, which has lain untouched for the last thirty years.

13 February 1957 I shall record only my personal experiences, nothing from hearsay or from newspapers—or if so, it will be noted as such. Yet it will, and must be, more than personal. For what is really personal? Do our thoughts fall from heaven, does a god endow us with feelings? Don't the masses think through us, the times feel through us? The reader will learn how a certain Just, Socialist Youth, soldier and officer under Hitler's banner,

Neulehrer* in the Soviet zone, member for six years of the SED Party apparatus, secretary-general of the German Writers' Union for a year, editor of *Sonntag* and now discharged from there, unemployed, frozen out of the political scene, what this Just was feeling and thinking in a period in which, for example, the author Willi Bredel wrote that he was in complete agreement with the policies of the Party as represented by Com. Ulbricht. I am not in agreement with them, and am convinced that there are many others who think the same.

I will be very careful not to say that out loud. But a human being can't stand always being alone with his thoughts. So I'm going to entrust them to these pages, to discreet paper that may yet one day speak out. I will not write this diary at home. Because I am afraid . . . afraid, that suddenly the door-bell will ring, and there will be six men standing outside holding a warrant for my arrest from the state's attorney "on strong suspicion of criminal activity," and that in searching my house they could find this little book containing my real thoughts. I am afraid of prison, though not of prison per se, heaven forbid! But to sit as a Communist in a Communist prison, having been charged or even convicted by a Communist court—the thought is unbearable. If one has to face one's class-enemies, everything is clear; one can fight or keep quiet if necessary. But here—who is the adversary, who is the enemy, against whom does one fight, when and why does one keep quiet? Even in the ten-hour interrogation, when I was at their mercy . . . but more of that later, everything in its proper sequence!

But I am not going to follow the chronological order of events exactly. First I must say where I am writing this diary: at my parents' in Bad Schmiedeberg. My father is ill; he deserved a peaceful old age with all his political dreams fulfilled. He is an old Communist, a founding member of the Czechoslovak Communist Party, and he surely does not agree with all my ideas. The old comrades tend not to be very receptive to new ideas. On the other hand, we of the younger generation must respect the wealth of experience of the older members, and take their warnings seriously, yet not canonize them. Marx didn't think out everything for Lenin, and Lenin left a lot of things for us. One can learn a lot from the

---

*Literally "new-teacher," refers to instructors in the Soviet zone of occupation who were hurriedly trained in 8-month courses to replace teachers suspected of affiliation with the Nazi Party.—Tr.

Ulbrichts, as long as they remain decent people. When they start employing Machiavellian techniques, however, and really provincial ones at that, one must turn one's back on them. That is exactly what worries the old Communists, the upstanding ones. They have Bebel's words in mind: watch your leaders' fingers! They do that, and see—dirty hands!

July 1989 So it happens that efforts at reform in the Communist movement are always intertwined with moral issues, indeed are frequently justified in moral terms. The Prague Spring of 1968 had as its goal "socialism with a human face." And it is precisely outrage over the violation of socialist and human principles that is driving people into opposition against their corrupt leaders, no matter how they later try to conceal their personal lust for power behind ostensible societal purposes. To preach water and drink wine—that's the epitome of hypocrisy!

13 February 1957 So here I am writing my diary—I've had all this in my head for a long time already, and here it will stay until the turning point has been passed. For it can truly be said that we have reached a turning point. Things are about to take a turn for the better. The opposition within the Party has no structure, no leadership, and no program, but it's there and growing. It can be combated and even held down, but not held back. It is the "new," asserting itself with elemental force according to the laws of dialectic. It is only this thought that gives me the strength and courage to hold on and not despair, for it is very difficult to live in such times. I can't sit by the water and go fishing, I can't live privately, I am a *zoon politikon*—their teaching was not lost on me, these men who today combat and condemn me.

July 1989 What a mad, child-like illusion! In extrapolating from circles I was moving in, I drew conclusions about the whole situation. Of a turning point there was nothing to be heard. On the contrary, with renewed vigor the conservatives exploited the events in Hungary to torpedo the reforms Khrushchev had introduced, until eventually they had toppled him. Soviet leaders and theoreticians today regret the development as misdirected, but at the time it overran and flattened us.

13 February 1957 Today it was reported in the papers that the Minister of State Security, Wollweber, in a speech to students in Berlin, announced that the counterrevolutionary activity by Harich, intended to bring about the downfall of socialism, had been verified by his statements, testimony from witnesses, and hand-written materials, none of which was disputed by Harich. Can one be that mistaken about somebody? I want to refrain from rash judgment and wait for the trial. To be sure, there were some things about Harich—exaggerations, inappropriate irony, half-playful brilliance out of sheer pleasure in coming up with original formulations, thinking and speaking in paradoxes in order to provoke people, something glittery and slippery—but eliminating socialism? And putting what in its place? I am filled with a deep suspicion of this investigation . . .

July 1989 *The irony of fate—one year later this same Wollweber, along with Schirdewan, was driven from the Party leadership, allegedly because they had neglected the struggle against "counterrevolutionary groups." What really lay behind it is impossible to know as long as the archives remain closed. I'll come back to this later.*

15 February 1957 But now to my entrance into the editorial ranks of *Sonntag*. It was in March 1955, two months after my departure from the administrative office of the Writers' Union. Jochen Mückenberger summoned me to the Culture Department of the Central Committee for a talk about my further deployment. I had a desire, I said, to work for a newspaper. *Sonntag* was proposed because they were short-handed, and I agreed. A few days later Becher invited me to come talk with him. It seemed acceptable to him to get me at the newspaper, which was considered his mouthpiece. He expressed his opinion that the paper had declined somewhat in significance, that the reputation of the newspaper had to be improved, specifically through the weight of the topics, the level on which they were treated, and the quality of the staff. I answered that I would undertake this assignment gladly and, I hoped, not without success. He had already spoken with Goeres, the editor in chief, Becher said, and I would be well received in the editorial offices. In parting, Becher hinted that my work as an editor would bring the project of the "Republic" closer to realization. This was an old plan of Becher's, in whose creation I had actively participated: a newspaper for the intelligentsia, on a high level and based on a broad alliance of humanistic and intellectual forces under the leadership of the Communists. The plan went back to the autumn of 1953, to the innocence of the New Course, when all buds were blooming and our world was full of hope . . .

July 1989   In the course of the autumn of 1955 this plan took on such clear contours that I was ordered to report to Sindermann, then directing the propaganda department of the Central Committee. Sindermann discussed with me the concept for this newspaper, which was to have a non-partisan, almost liberal character. Budzislavski would be the editor in chief, while I would take over the culture section. We were supposed to develop plans for it while at Sonntag, *which was apparently then destined to be folded into this new newspaper. We designed the layout in the editorial office, agreed upon a format like Karl Marx's* Rheinische Zeitung, *with at least sixteen pages—it would have undoubtedly been an interesting newspaper, an advocate of democratization and liberalization of the system—budding dreams, which like so many others were never allowed to ripen . . .*

15 February 1957   I was received by the editorial staff with what seemed to be a certain constraint. Goeres I knew from my work in the Central Committee; he had even been assigned to me for training. Goeres is a good journalist but lacks a fixed point of view; nevertheless, I believe that in the long run we would have worked well together. I learned that among the non-Party colleagues like Joho, Piltz, and Netzeband the fear had arisen that I had been installed among them as a sort of political commissar—which in light of recent developments seems like a bad joke.

In Goeres' office, which would later become mine, I met Heinz Zöger, a dry man possessing several curious qualities, which I attributed to certain complexes. After a somewhat protracted mutual sizing-up we achieved a friendly working relationship.

To my surprise they both offered me the position of fine arts editor. Mückenberger and Becher had always spoken of my being in charge of the culture section, that is, art, literature, theater, music. It seemed as if Goeres and Zöger wanted to test me first. They were afraid, as I later learned, that I was a stubborn and dogmatic person; at any rate this reputation was supposed to have preceded me from my work in the Central Committee—while they actually subscribed to very "liberal" ideas. Zöger emphasized the concept of "positive impatience" with which the editorial posture and working style was to be defined. A critical attitude toward reality from the viewpoint of objective possibilities; struggle against the petty-bourgeois shortsightedness that disfigures socialism; free, open discussion; in short: a New Course. I was in complete agreement and ran my department, "Fine Arts," in this spirit.

The first weeks in the editorial offices were a happy time for me. The work did not unduly tax my strength, and an open and cheerful atmosphere prevailed among my colleagues; they were for the most part undogmatic, creative people. We had successes, circulation increased steadily, distinguished new people joined the staff: Herbert Jhering, Heinz Kamnitzer, Stephan Hermlin, Kurt Schifner, Karl-Heinz Reutter, and others. Dealings with the directors of the publishing house, which had hitherto suffered from petty frictions, improved visibly, as did our relationship with the secretary of the Cultural League. We mounted vigorous attacks on anything plushy and kitschy. If today no one disputes that socialist art has to be modern art, it is due to our efforts. We took an extremely critical position towards pseudo-classicism in architecture, something that did not exactly win us the friendship of Kurt Liebknecht (then president of the Bauakademie) and probably aroused Ulbricht's antagonism toward us even then. On the other hand we won the support of many architects, starting with Henselmann . . .

Goeres left in the summer. The Party had begun proceedings against him for alleged moral deviations. The result: relegation to the applicant list. I protested this punishment as too severe, but the Regional Party Control Commission upheld the decision. In addition it seemed advisable for him to get some rest, for health reasons. Zöger and I planned to sign him on as a freelance in charge of the fine arts section, but there we ran into a brick wall with the publishers and the Cultural League. Goeres had lost all favor with them, and they insisted on cutting him off completely.

It was decided that a triumvirate would direct the newspaper: Heinz Zöger, Gustav Just, and Otto Distler. This last member had been recommended to us by Günter Caspar, who knew him from his work at the *Tägliche Rundschau*. Distler was a competent journalist and a well-read and cultured intellectual, but very difficult as a person, so that there was often friction with him. In his criticism of Zöger's high-handedness he was not, as I later realized, completely wrong, but in general he caused us many troubled hours.

He had left again by the end of the year.

Unwelcome Trips Abroad

In early summer we began an energetic campaign to expand travel to friendly neighboring countries. Many people, naturally also intellectuals, suffered under the restrictions of our country. One could travel abroad, but for the most part only on official assignments as part of a delegation. You couldn't blame people for wanting to go to the Tatras or the Balkans on their own. We went ahead and developed concrete proposals to solve this problem of foreign exchange—but it didn't turn out well for us.

The bone of contention was an article on the question of travel abroad which Hans Jürgen Jessel had written. It was during my summer vacation. As I read the article in Ahrenshoop, even I was put out by the pervasive tone of dissatisfaction and certain inappropriate parallels to West Germany.

But others were put out even more. The secretariat of the Central Commission occupied itself with us and instructed the Commission on Agitation to "occupy" itself with us likewise. So we had to put in an appearance before Horst Sindermann. It was the usual song and dance, with demands issued, on ideological principle. Emil Dusika distinguished himself especially by his show of cleverness. Apparently we did not understand that we were to write for the intelligentsia the way they were supposed to think. Instead we were mirroring the mood of the intelligentsia, giving in to it, thereby legitimizing it. It was the same old song: the Party, viz. the existing Party leadership, knows exactly what is right, what is to be thought, and all comrades have the duty to propagate this viewpoint. I tried during the discussion to raise the objection that the press did not merely have a duty to popularize the familiar, that which was considered correct, but also to help recognize the unfamiliar, help solve the unsolved, etc. Otherwise the Party leadership would not have to read any newspapers. In reality, however, the Party and state leadership did have to read their own newspapers to see what new thoughts and problems were surfacing among the masses. What repercussions of their decisions and decrees were manifesting themselves? What did the people affected by their measures think of them?

But I did not get anywhere with this argument, because on this question, like others, the democrats were at odds with the Party bureaucrats. They let us have it with both barrels, yet it seemed to me that none of those involved had deep feelings about it, not even Horst Sindermann, who settled the matter as if it were an irksome duty.

Zöger cleared up the affair in an inappropriately crude manner. He wrote a caustic article attacking Jessel, without, however, naming him. Offended, Jessel turned his back on us, which I, at least, always deeply regretted.

Organizing Your Vacation
(excerpt)
. . . Let us address in the abstract the general issue of vacationing. How would we like to spend our vacation? How can we spend our vacation? Can we always spend our vacation as we would like to? Tastes are known to differ, in love as in cooking, as well as in the "shaping" of a vacation. Unfortunately, it often seems that this fact is not so universally acknowledged as could be desired, especially among those who arrange the organization of our vacations. Organization of vacations? How soon I'm stopped!* Is it really that necessary, can't we take care of it ourselves, each for himself? Certain things must be looked after, that goes without saying, but one cannot shake off the feeling from time to time that it is being somewhat overdone.

First of all: we do not want to be unfair. The FDGB can't give us trips down the Rhine, nor can it create vacation hostels out of thin air. But it can do something about the way vacations are organized in the existing hostels. It seems to be a widespread childhood disease of our times that one can unexpectedly fall under suspicion of individualism, but it happens in few places as quickly as at a vacation hostel. Zealous hostel directors, aspiring to recreate the carefree days of childhood, create the broadest possible bases for a happy vacation, from collective hikes to jolly "Old Home Nights." Anyone who does not participate, who thinks the indiscriminately assembled population of a vacation hostel is not even supposed to

---

*Johann W. Goethe, *Faust, Part I*, edited and translated by Stuart Atkins, (Boston: Suhrkamp/Insel, 1984), p. 33.

form a collective, who thinks a collective is also not a herd of sheep, this person reveals himself as an individualist, a loner, a social outsider tainted with petty-bourgeois vestiges. Such types have already been suitably branded, or to be more precise, castigated in the extraordinarily cheerful films produced by DEFA, as well as in similar short stories, whose authors and actors have never spent a vacation in a FDGB hostel.

So let us have a little less organizing. Leave the people in peace. Some people actually feel the need to be alone during their vacation or to strike up their own acquaintances. Things are structured for them the rest of the year, after all.

Last but not least, lest we neglect anyone, a word to those one could call the incurable optimists. They will not stop hoping that someday they may see a bit of the world. But not as a member of a delegation, also not as a vacation guest who, transported to Varna without his passport, puts in his required time on the beach. They want to travel. But that's asking too much. By the way, they want to pay for their trips themselves, specifically with the money they earned by performing outstandingly their duties to our Republic.

Let us say it openly: this is an unsatisfactory state of affairs, and no one understands exactly why it has to be like this. At any rate, in dealing with the relevant agencies one easily gets the impression that some of their staff members need to shake off the complex that makes them see a potential spy in every traveler who goes abroad. Past experience proves that spies achieve their goals through other means, assuming they have not been in our midst long since. Perhaps it would even do our state apparatus good to give up some of its organizational tasks. Travel bureaus could do an excellent job here. And since recently even people from Dr. Adenauer's Federal Republic have been allowed to visit certain peoples' democracies, the citizens of the peace-loving German Democratic Republic may perhaps continue to hope.

Anon.

—*Sonntag*, 7 October 1955

July 1989 At that time the issue was travel to other socialist countries, a topic that was no longer an issue a few years later, with travel to Czechoslovakia and Poland even becoming visa-free. Since then new complications have arisen: Hungary has opened her borders, so that restrictions can certainly be expected. Today the far more burning issue is the understandable desire to travel to Western countries. The stifling restrictions here, the lack of knowledge of the world, are increasingly felt by the youth as oppressive. A recent decree has laid down exactly who has to be related to whom, and for what reason he can visit him. Try to imagine such a law in the Imperial Reich or the Weimar Republic! How the liberals and the left would have poured derision on an order that violates the most natural of human rights in such a fashion! Today, however, such an arrangement is hailed by even the Western democracies as "a step in the right direction."

And my opinion of the role of the press at that time was identical to what in the Soviet Union is now called "glasnost." Reading the present-day Soviet press is a delight. To it nothing is taboo. Ruthlessly it uncovers abuses, brings up problems that were swept under the rug for decades, and exposes to the light of day dark episodes of the past. New thinking—while we're still stuck in the same old rut.

Friends in Prague

15 February 1957   During this period we established a correspondence with the *Literární noviny* in Prague and agreed upon an exchange of editors in order to promote mutual cooperation. In September of 1955 I went to Prague. There I found friends in every sense of the word—Communists working and struggling under the same circumstances. They had to deal with the same myopic functionaries and narrow-minded dogmatists as we did. Like us, they had an image of a different, freer intellectual and cultural life. They advocated, like us, an exchange of views on unresolved questions, but they spoke much more openly and extensively than we, who were always looking over our shoulders. The writers, but other intellectuals as well, took part to a much greater degree in the discussion of the current intellectual situation. They were farther along than we, and I was actually seized by envy, a creative envy that spurred me on.

And that was nothing compared to Poland! In Prague I met Richard Matuszewski, one of the editors of *Nowa Kultura*. In Poland at that time there were spirited discussions about the "Poem for Adults" by Adam Wazyk. To think it was even possible to publish such a poem! "Yes," said Matuszewski, "that did not happen by itself. We had to fight for it, we Communist writers and publishers."

One has to be bolder in fighting for the truth and freeing literature and art from the dogmas of the past. With this intention in mind, I returned from Prague. And Ludvík Vesely, who then visited us, helped me spread this idea among the editorial staff.

July 1989   Yes, my friends from Literární—*Vesely, Sergei Machonin, Jan Pilár, and the rest of them. Their paper played an important role in preparing the way for the Prague Spring of 1968. And after the invasion of the Warsaw Pact troops they paid dearly for it. Pilár got out just in time, was allowed to continue working, and today still directs the Ceskovslovensky spisovatel publishing house. The newspaper was banned, but later appeared under the name* Listy *and published the famous "2,000 Words," the manifesto for a liberal and democratic socialism that was signed by virtually every important intellectual.* Listy *was also banned. Ludvík Vesely emigrated. Machonin had to eke out his life as a night watchman in the national museum. What became of him and the other editors, I do not know. What was starting to take shape in 1955 was international cooperation by reform-minded Communists, something of which today there is hardly a trace.*

Our Discussion of Music

16 February 1957   While in the area of literature things had at least begun to move in connection with preparations for the Writers' Congress, while new questions and proposals had been surfacing in the fine arts for some time, the world of music remained completely stagnant. At the end of 1955 it was decided in the editorial offices at my suggestion to initiate discussion of musical matters. The impetus came from a conversation I had with Paul Dessau in Halle, in the apartment of then General Musical Director, Horst-Tanu Margraf. Paul Dessau began to swear furiously at our "Music Czars," who so unfortunately opposed modernism and with their doctrinaire Zhdanov dogma were impeding rather than supporting the development of socialist music. I urged Dessau to write something about it, and he agreed.

It turned out to be harder than we had thought. I visited him several times in his apartment in Zeuthen, to advise him about the wording of the article. He showed the final version to Brecht. We also let Wohlgemuth, Schwaen, and Cilensek see it, all of whom, except for Cilensek, who dodged the issue, immediately wrote complementary articles.

So in January 1956 we were able to publish an entire page on "The State of Our Musical Life." It hit like a bombshell, for so many taboos were violated, so much was expressed publicly that had hitherto been thought only in private.

Everyone reacted differently. Ernst Hermann Meyer, whom I had taken for a mediocre composer but a good musicologist and an honorable man, was offended and wrote us a letter in which he addressed me with the formal "Sie" and informed us that he would not take part in the discussion. During a debate at the Academy of the Arts he described *Sonntag* as a tabloid for which no upstanding person could work.

Wagner-Régeny, Buttig, Spiess and others expressed to me their gratification at our initiating discussion and promised to participate. Hanns Eisler told one of our editors that he found the first articles good and that he would have something to say later on. "You have to keep at least one big gun in reserve in case the discussion develops further and the heavy artillery has to be brought up," he said.

But the discussion did not develop any further—it was choked off; heavy artillery was no longer necessary, which, I believe, even Hanns Eisler, if he can forgive me, did not wholly object to.

The Composers' Union counterattacked, held meetings and advised its obedient members not to continue the discussion in *Sonntag* because such matters belonged in the Union mouthpiece *Musik und Gesellschaft*. They also attempted to make us look ridiculous, whereupon I dashed off an appropriate response. Then they, too, took offense. Eberhard Rebling, who had previously sought my friendship and of whom I was quite fond, treated me with emphatically cool contempt when we met at the opening of the "House of Czechoslovak Culture." As I jokingly tried to bridge the gap between us, he said: "Your discussion has served a good purpose. It has created publicity for *Musik und Gesellschaft*." I was no slouch, and, admittedly not very tactful; I promptly printed this comment as the quotation of the day. That really did it.

Rudolf Herzog, the idiotic and conceited adjutant to Paul Wandel, came up to me in a theater and said that we should put an end to this stupid discussion of music. At that point I finally realized which way the wind was blowing.

The Fourth German Writers' Congress

While I was still active in the Writers' Union we had begun making preparations for the Congress. The first date chosen was March 1954; then it was postponed to the fall. Having already postponed it once, they postponed it again from March 1955 to the beginning of February 1956. It was never clear to me why the Central Committee found this date as well as the next one premature. There was something behind it, of course: in the Central Committee there were fears that the writers might actually be unruly and bring up questions for which answers were not available. The same old story: only those questions can be asked for which the leadership has a ready answer, because it is infallible and must therefore know everything. Who would dare suggest that they should seek the people's advice—rather than always giving advice! Learn from the masses! is a frequently used slogan, but for now not more than that.

The other side of things: despite all the encouragement, only a pitiful and hesitant literary discussion occurred. I made a point of calling for it with my friends at *Sonntag*, as did the members of the Culture Department of the Central Committee. As it turned out later, however, we had different things in mind: we wanted writers finally to speak out publicly about some problems that moved them deeply: writing the truth, freedom of artistic expression, ending dogmatic thought-control, abandoning Party-line aesthetics. The CC, however, wanted and had understood the necessary discussion to entail speaking out against precisely these "liberal" tendencies, so that the partisan role of literature in assisting with problems of daily political life could be clearly demonstrated. They found their man in Wilhelm Girnus, who with his characteristic walrus-mustached style of heavy-handedness raised ideology to a position of preeminence while derogating artistic mastery to the position of handmaiden. As might have been expected, the response came from Walther Victor, who valiantly put himself in the position of defending mastery. This led to a vapid dispute, which although carried out loudly and not without casualties, was vapid because it focused only on words and concepts and did not penetrate to any depth. There should have been a clear and unmistakable proclamation before and during the congress of the right and duty of the author to operate in the vanguard of the present, to tackle unresolved contradictions, to do more than embellish and illustrate the decrees of the Party and regime. Our literature will remain sterile and uninteresting so long as its creators do not have the right to tread upon the new thematic, spiritual, intellectual, and political ground that opens up daily in the course of building socialism.

The congress was set up in such a way, however, that no serious analysis of the fairly pathetic state of our contemporary literature could be broached. The theme of Becher's keynote address was the greatness of our literature. This greatness revealed itself even in his address to reside more in the indisputably greater perspective than in any greatness of the literary works themselves.

Georg Lukács, as respondent, therefore had good reason to speak about correct and incorrect perspectives. What his words came to was this: no more prettying things up, no more passing off dream as reality, instead writing the truth, and therefore realistically. Ernst Bloch also spoke along those lines, taking special aim at superrationalism in literary theory. Even the loyal Bredel took up a position against Girnus, although his response was very wishy-washy and more emotional.

All this brought on an appearance by W. Ulbricht, who, to everyone's amazement, took the podium at the conference and trotted out timeworn truisms. The unmistakable intention of his words was to counter every possible "liberalization."

In his speech Ulbricht also made a critical, unfortunately not very clear reference to *Sonntag*, suggesting that the people there had not yet understood the nature of the struggle, but were still paddling along in the same old channels.

The affair left Zöger and me no peace. At the congress's conclusion all the participants gathered at a reception hosted by Becher. Grotewohl and Ulbricht were present. I had a good conversation with Konstantin Fedin, from whose circumspect hints I deduced that intellectual life in the Soviet Union had also begun to move. Then I saw Ulbricht talking to Abusch. I grabbed Zöger and we went over to them. Ulbricht turned away just then, so I hastily asked Abusch to introduce us.

"We are the two comrades from *Sonntag*," I began. "We heard that you, Comrade Ulbricht, were criticizing us, and we would like to know the particulars."

He laughed; he was altogether in a splendid mood that evening. "Everyone makes mistakes," he said, "but with you people it's not that you make mistakes. You have the wrong line!"

We protested and tried to explain our mission to him, that we were trying to apply the Party line in our special area and so on, but everything bounced off his self-assured condescending smile. "You have not yet understood that the New Course is over." When we pointed out that we also had West German intellectuals in mind, he cut us off, saying that we had other organs of the press for that.

The New Course was over? I thought it was just beginning in earnest. If that was his line, well we certainly did have another. It was clear that evening that Ulbricht and the CC were not criticizing this or that mistake, but that the whole direction did not suit them. I am convinced today that Ulbricht went along with every step of the New Course against his will, always with the fixed belief that he would find an opportunity to return to the old hard line. He is a man of the hard line; I do not have confidence that he can carry out the new politics of democratization with real conviction. Every word in this direction comes out of his mouth reluctantly and doesn't ring true, but rather as if it were squeezed out of him by circumstances. The people do not believe him either, this exponent of a policy based on the bayonet and the tank, not on the trust of the masses.

The New Course

By early summer 1953 our political situation had become unbearable. The workers had been seized with a deep dissatisfaction. Badly thought-out and foolish measures had made them angry—arbitrary increases in production quotas, reductions in or elimination of the workers' weekly commuter tickets, price increases for jam(!). The middle class felt as though it was about to go under. Restaurant proprietors and small retailers were no longer receiving ration-cards. Creative artists were groaning under ever-increasing intellectual pressure. The population was responding to the precipitous pace of socialization by fleeing the Republic in droves.

At that time I was working as a section head in the Culture Department of the CC and frequently came in contact with artists, especially those in the Academy, and I kept hearing of their dissatisfaction. In February I wrote a comprehensive report on it to Hans Lauter, secretary of the CC for cultural issues, as well as informing Comrade Beburov of the SMA (Soviet Military Administration). All this gave rise to a discussion involving several Academy members and Holtzhauer and his people from the State Commission on the Arts. Magritz and Girnus were playing a nefarious role at the time. Yet reason made deep inroads even into the Culture Department itself. Becher, with whom I often had lunch at the Club for Creative Artists, frequently criticized it. As things developed, the Arts Commission became the representative of the hard line, while the Academy of the Arts emerged as a center of opposition.

Then came the business with the Marx-Cantata about Cuba by Forest. Forest had composed it using texts from the "Poem on Man." It was performed at the major Karl Marx Festival and caused quite a scandal. The secretariat of the CC adopted a resolution condemning the work as formalistic, and Egon Rentzsch, director of the Culture Department, was relieved of his duties. We were subjected to the usual meetings in order to "eliminate once and for all opportunistic and conciliatory behavior from the Culture Department."

At Easter I had a talk with Rentzsch at his apartment. He warned me to be very careful not to fall victim to the two hit-men, Willi Adam and Rudolf Herzog, who had brought him down. Apparently Rentzsch considered the resolution an injustice, which in fact it was. We parted as good friends, convinced that one day this injustice would be rectified.

Shortly thereafter they also came after me—as an opportunist, conciliator, liberal. I defended myself as best I could. Adam let something slip out: "Egon Rentzsch said that you are a conciliator and that it was chiefly under your influence that he was pushed into his mistakes!" Oh boy, I thought, and probed until it came out: good old Egon had actually expressed himself along these lines before the Party leadership, had acknowledged their resolution to be correct, had welcomed his dismissal, and proposed that mine be effectuated soon. That a man could be so two-faced—a man who had stood up to the Nazis for twelve years in prison and a concentration camp! His behavior was rewarded a few years later when he was recalled to Berlin to be secretary of the FDGB.

Hans Lauter accordingly felt compelled to drop his plan of proposing me as director of the Culture Department, a plan he had revealed to me earlier. The leadership was provisionally entrusted to Jochen Mückenberger along with Rudolf Herzog.

I was therefore all the more surprised when in May 1953 I was invited to meetings held in great secrecy. They involved a commission of the Central Committee that was chaired by Fred Oelssner and included: Paul Wandel, minister and director of the Office for Coordination of Cultural Issues, Else Zaisser, minister for national education, Kurt Hager, director of the Propaganda Department, Willi Barth, the Central Committee's consultant on religion. Lauter was, if I remember correctly, no longer the secretary. Wandel was already the new man for cultural affairs. The commission had the assignment of proposing to the Politburo measures in the area of culture and propaganda for a new political course. We discussed the situation with unprecedented candor. Everything I was objecting to was criticized. I really came to life and felt in my element. The connection with the masses was supposed to be restored, unreasonable and rash measures rescinded, greater freedoms made possible. The winds of change since Malenkov's coming to power were blowing from Moscow.

I could not get over my astonishment at how open-minded and reasonable comrades like Oelssner, Wandel, and Hager sounded, how precisely informed they were about the "belly-aches" of the intellectuals, how very willing they were to do things differently. Are these comrades surprised today that I cannot take it seriously when they talk as they used to? Which is their true face, the one from early June 1953, or the one of today, 1957? And why did they bring me into this commission, me of all people from the Culture Department? Did they know that I am wholeheartedly a man of the New Course, that I hold and will hold all other policies to be incorrect?

On the ninth of June the Party came out with its new program, but it was announced by the same leaders who had previously pushed through the old course. That was unwise. Ulbricht should have been reined in; he could have remained in the Politburo, but not as secretary-general. The change in course came too suddenly, and people didn't believe us. But I knew they were serious about it in the Central Committee, and above all our Soviet comrades were serious about it.

July 1989 The factor that triggered a new policy in the socialist countries was of course Stalin's death in March 1953. We have since learned from documents what went on at the time, how the "survivors" fought for power among themselves, how at first a troika was set up, until Khrushchev, after the liquidation of Beria and the neutralization of Malenkov, emerged as the new dictator. Evidently they had a new conception of the German question, about which I can only speculate. In the GDR there was supposed to be no more talk of building socialism; reunification was considered more seriously. Ulbricht made it seem after Beria's downfall that Beria had been the only one who wanted to give up the GDR. What was really going on at that time can be revealed only by the real insiders. My firm conviction is that Rudolf Herrnstadt was viewed by the Soviets as the up-and-coming man, and the fact that Zaisser, the minister for state security, was later reprimanded for being an opponent of Ulbricht, confirms my suspicion that Beria was calling many of the shots.

16 February 1957 The whole thing had not been thoroughly thought out. Uncertainties arose, and there was much talk of merely making concessions to the petty bourgeois backwardness of the masses. People spoke about socialism only in whispers, as if the New Course were not intended to bring about a better implementation of socialism.

Two examples of how this confusion went straight to the top: the presiding council of the Cultural League held a conference at the beginning of June dedicated to the memory of Karl Marx. I gave a talk on Marx's relationship to art and literature (later published). On orders of the Central Committee we speakers were not to mention socialism in the GDR. I had a tiff with Jochen Mückenberger because someone told him that we should even distance ourselves from the term "socialist realism!"

The second example concerns my little book *Marx, Engels, Lenin, and Stalin on Art and Literature*, which just then was being prepared for publication by the Dietz-Verlag. At the demand of the publishing house I had to delete all references to the building of socialism, which made the last part of the essay sheer drivel.

Apparently at that time extremely far-reaching notions existed among the Soviets and our Party leadership. Thus Oelssner said at a conference of the above-mentioned commission that we had to take care that in pan-German elections in the foreseeable future some positions remained in our hands. We would have to operate as agitators to counter the Social Democrats (he named Ollenhauer)*, who would speak at rallies in Halle and Leipzig.

---

*Erich Ollenhauer, head of the Social Democratic Party in West Germany after Kurt Schumacher.—Tr.

The 17th of June

Much has been said and written about this black day in the history of the German workers' movement, but in reality far too little. The best and truest things were said at the 14th plenary session of the Central Committee, which convened shortly thereafter. Later everything people said was increasingly embellished, even, I would say, falsified. Obviously there can be no doubt that the reactionaries had their hand in that, as in Poland, as in Hungary. But that is only a part of the truth, and I believe almost a minor one.

The main question is this: how, in a workers' and peasants' dictatorship, can the workers and peasants be against it, reject the Party leadership and go their own way, a way that in part leads them into the clutches of the reactionaries? We have not yet received an answer to this question in connection with the 17th of June.

My experiences on this day: we were having a department meeting on the 16th in our rooms in the House of the National Council on Thälmannplatz. Our secretary rushed in: "There's a rally, a demonstration, in front of the government building on Leipziger Strasse!"

What was so special about that, we answered unsuspectingly; rallies were quite common.

Yes, but this one wasn't for us; shouting could be heard.

So we went over there immediately; it was barely two minutes away. The square in front of the House of the Ministries was filled with two or three thousand construction workers in white overalls; they had come directly from their building sites. They were standing, sitting, and squatting in dense clusters, for the most part embittered and angry, some of them also cocky, amused at the goings-on. They did not give anyone who was well-dressed a chance to speak. Several of them promptly offered me, with my glasses, "one right in the kisser." We had no idea why they were standing here, what was actually happening. The square was seething with conversations and shouting, until gradually chanting began. Ulbricht or Grotewohl should come out, they demanded.

Then a man jumped up onto a raised platform, probably a table; it was Prof. Havemann, and he began to speak to the workers. They didn't listen and shouted him down. Then Minister Fritz Selbmann tried it. He held up his hands, a worker's hands, to show them that he was one of them. But they didn't give him a chance to speak either. I had the impression that there were organized rabble-rousers among them who had gained a hearing because the construction workers were extremely upset about the raising of quotas.

Some of them dispersed in the course of the afternoon, the rest marched in a column back to the Stalinallee. We did not give the matter further thought, believing it to have been taken care of. The Party leadership, which had more than once let itself be caught by surprise, was basking, I believe, in the same illusion.

That same evening a meeting of Party activists took place in the Friedrichstadtpalast, where Grotewohl and Ulbricht presented the New Course. I was there with KuBa and Rudi Engel, who wanted to celebrate my birthday at our place afterwards. The Party leaders also mentioned the demonstration by the construction workers, but really only in passing. There was a lesson to be learned; we had to explain the New Course to the workers, and so on and so forth. Privately I expected—with some annoyance, I have to admit; it was, after all, my birthday—that we would be kept there, immediately dispatched to the factories with night shifts to mobilize Party groups or something like that. But nothing of the sort happened.

We then drove home in KuBa's car. As we crossed the Marx-Engels-Platz we encountered a column of trucks filled with *Volkspolizei.* "Aha," I said with satisfaction to KuBa, "they will hermetically block off the border so that no West Berliners can come over, then nothing can happen." But that was also a deluded hope. The borders were not blocked.

My party went on until four in the morning. Peter Brock from Halle was also there; he had discussions to conduct the next day. The telephone woke me at 8 o'clock. I was to come into the department at once; there was something going on that could not be explained over the phone.

We left right away, Peter and I. A strange restlessness was apparent as soon as we got to the street and even more on the elevated municipal railway: masses of workers, whom one otherwise never saw at this time of day, were riding into the city with grim, determined faces. In Schöneweide we saw columns of them on foot heading downtown. Then we heard from several corners of the train compartment the words "general strike." Past the Eastern Station the streets were black with people, as were the platforms. We got out at Friedrichstrasse and parted ways; Peter wanted to go to the Henschel-Verlag. All traffic was at a standstill. Friedrichstrasse and Unter den Linden were overflowing with masses of people shoving aimlessly back and forth. There was not a lot of yelling to be heard. Here and there groups formed around a comrade who was trying to get a discussion going. That was, however, as I soon realized, a hopeless undertaking. Feelings were running too high for people to listen to any reasoned argument.

On instructions from above my comrades from the department and I went out to agitate. We were all convinced of the senselessness of it. It was as if we had been given the order to scoop out the Scharmützelsee with a teaspoon . . .

Around noon a terrific rain came down, but even this, contrary to my hopes, was not able to cool off feelings. Then a state of emergency was proclaimed, Soviet tanks rolled through the streets, people were called upon to disperse, and so far as I could tell, they obeyed. Most of them had been following no program, only their general dissatisfaction. I did not get the impression that the mass of the workers, for it was mainly workers, were demonstrating against socialism. They only wanted it understood that we had to close the book on certain methods once and for all, which the Party for its part had already actually done with the transition to the New Course.

July 1989 *Since then thirty-six years have passed, and opinions on the 17th of June are still divided. The Stalinists speak of it as a counterrevolutionary, even fascist putsch, while in the West it is called the people's uprising and celebrated as the Day of German Unity. Both explanations are neither wholly true nor untrue. The uprising of the construction workers on the 16th of June was spontaneous, no doubt about that. The tinder of dissatisfaction was so widespread that a spark sufficed to ignite a blaze. That the fire spread to the entire GDR by the 17th was surely due to the fact that RIAS immediately reported in detail on the events in Berlin. It seems unlikely to me that organized, illegal forces methodically planned the demonstration and other actions. In any case the Party and state leadership of the GDR never presented any conclusive evidence. To be sure, thousands were thrown into prison and labeled the ringleaders of the strike, but it was never publicly proven that any of them had been acting on instructions from the West. That, as always with such popular uprisings, hooligans and asocial elements found their way in and got involved was not surprising. There was arson, convicted Nazi war criminals were let out of prisons, Party members were beaten up or otherwise harassed; but that does not determine the overall character of the event.*

What was, however, much more important and fateful was this: because of the 17th of June Ulbricht and his people, who had already started to be pushed aside, recovered their position of power. This is what you get for easing up on things, they said to their opponents. We have no reason to celebrate the 17th of June as a glorious day. Without it the New Course would have brought radical changes, and Ulbricht's days as the first man in the Party would have been numbered. Thus history acts out its macabre drama time and again: the demonstrators wanted to bring down Ulbricht, but, on the contrary, they helped him stay in power, more impervious than before.

16 February 1957 I set off optimistically for my summer vacation (July 1953), leaving directly from a Central Committee meeting held at the beginning of July and chaired by Paul Wandel. Once again the representatives of the Academy of the Arts under the leadership of Becher sat facing their hostile brothers from the State Arts Commission. Becher minced no words. In a few programmatic points the Academy had presented its views on the New Course in cultural policy. Among other things, a marked reduction in state involvement in the arts was demanded. The presiding council of the Cultural League had taken a similar position.

Brecht had at that time published two biting poems addressed to the Arts Commission and the Office for Literature. Harich had written a very pointed article against the arts administration, in which, to be sure, he focused so exclusively on our internal contradictions that he ignored the external contradictions of the class struggle. But it was unmistakable that long pent-up bitterness was being vented. I was often appalled at the hatred with which some artists came out against people like Girnus and Magritz.

A fierce adversary of Becher's at the above-mentioned meeting was Ernst Hoffman. In the excitement he repeatedly called Becher "Brecher" (lumping him together with Brecht), until finally Becher interjected: "He doesn't even know our names, he mixes everything up, Becher and Brecht, and a creature like that formulates cultural policy!"

This is what I think today: if we had given consideration to the Academy's proposals and carried out the recommended measures, we could have spared ourselves a lot of discussion after the Twentieth Party Congress. As it was, there was a displeased reaction, a tendency to pull back whenever possible; the Ministry of Culture was set up under the direction of Becher to be sure, but with Holtzhauer's people. Halfway measures . . .

Holtzhauer's dismissal, demanded by all the artists, ran into resistance at the top. And why not: Holtzhauer had merely carried out the policies of the Party; he was Ulbricht's man. I heard that Ulbricht spoke out in the Secretariat against Holtzhauer's removal from office, and I would not be surprised if dear Helmuth soon rose again to new glory.

July 1989 *Holtzhauer was personally a man of integrity, a proven antifascist whom the Nazis had imprisoned for a long time. His activities as director of the Art Commission do not earn him much credit. His later years as director of the National Research Center and Historic Sites in Weimar are, however, commendable, which shows how Communists, once freed from the pressure of Stalinist dictatorship, can manifest their true, essentially humanistic nature.*

The New Course Is Hammered Into Shape

16 February 1957 Everything happened differently than I had imagined. I had thought we would now discuss the New Course in all cultural organizations—and in the political realm too, of course—and consider measures that would really win the artists over to our side. In the course of this process of self-examination, I thought, some comrades who were especially truculent champions of the old course would naturally have to practice self-criticism, and a few of them, who were not ready or willing to change their thinking, would have to be dismissed.

Yet after the 15th and 16th plenary sessions of the CC, it was those who had always stood for what was now called "the New Course" who now had to practice self-criticism, myself of course included. After the 17th of June, insofar as anyone within the Party was considered at fault, the blame fell not on those who had alienated the Party from the masses through their policies, but on those who wanted to see a lesson in the events. Herrnstadt and Zaisser were condemned and frozen out. Nobody but the members of the Politburo knows to this day what Herrnstadt's real intentions were. From a few of the phrases in Ulbricht's speech that dealt with this issue I suspect that his ideas were not deviant in the slightest: renewal of the Party, overcoming the omnipotence of the apparatus. At that time there might have been for once an opportunity to discuss within the Party the problems that affect every honorable, thinking Communist. That was blocked, just as it is being blocked today.

To me this systematic retraction of the New Course was a bitter disappointment that began to shake my faith in Ulbricht as leader of the Party. I could not ward off the suspicion that all his people had merely gone through the motions of cooperating with the New Course, that they had never grasped its true nature. For them these were concessions that had been wrung from them in a moment of weakness. They were waiting for the first favorable moment to regain the upper hand and halt the process or even reverse it. That the New Course was connected with a renaissance, a renewal of humaneness, with a different, more self-effacing relationship to the masses—that they did not understand. And I believe that some of them will never understand the new political situation . . .

How else could Ulbricht have directed us to terminate the New Course in February 1956, one month before the Twentieth Party Congress of the Soviet Communist Party? He considered these policies tactical maneuvers, though at the time he asserted something different.

July 1989 How little has changed in the leadership of the SED! With the same reluctance or even flat-out rejection they are responding to the new thinking propagated by Gorbachev and developed and articulated by Soviet theoreticians and publicists.

My days in the Culture Department were numbered—I was not wanted there anymore, and I felt I had to get out of the apparatus. They nevertheless offered me a golden opportunity. Becher suggested that I replace Rudi Engel as director of the Academy of the Arts; Engel would then take over duties in the Foreign Ministry. KuBa felt, however, that this position was more suitable for older people, not for a young, dynamic comrade, which I was considered at the time. He saw to it that I was nominated to be secretary-general of the Writers' Union and elected by the Union's steering committee. I immediately got rid of the title secretary-general. I

*brought organizational discipline into the Union's apparatus, which
KuBa had directed in a downright chaotic fashion. There are many
interesting things that could be written about my activities there,
but let's stay with the topic and get back to* Sonntag.

The Uproar over *The Lützower*

16 February 1957 Before I go on to the decisive event (the
Twentieth Party Congress), I must still mention our controversy
with Hedda Zinner.* She had written a mediocre play about 1813
(*The Lützower*), which was performed with modest success at the
Deutsches Theater around New Year's 1956. The experts expressed
violent criticism of the play's treatment of history as well as the
dramaturgy. Jhering wrote a negative review in *Sonntag*. I myself
never saw the play, only read it, and found it dubious just from the
reading.

Hedda Zinner came flying at me like a fury at the Writers' Union
Congress. How could we have allowed her play to be discussed in
such a derogatory way, and by Jhering, that . . . There followed
insults which I no longer remember. I tried to appease the enraged
dramatist with the suggestion that we could also organize a
discussion of Jhering's review, but the woman was not to be calmed
down.

In the meantime she had probably driven everyone crazy, for a
few days later we were called to the Culture Department of the
CC, where serious charges were made against us because of this
incident. At *Sonntag* we set up a Party meeting where our theater
policy could be discussed. Hilderose Boockh and Hans Grümmer
from the Culture Department represented the Department's critical
viewpoint, altogether rather moderately and unfortunately not too
competently. On our side stood Max Schroeder, managing editor of
the Aufbau-Verlag, who also took a dim view of *The Lützower*. We
should not concede a monopoly to Jhering, the comrades from the
CC demanded. That we knew ourselves. We had for a long time
been looking for a second critic, a Marxist. We should not favor

---

*An East German artist known for following Party guidelines on art with
the strictest obedience.—Tr.

Brecht so exclusively—yes, but what if his theater actually was and is the best!

We then received a letter from the physician Prof. Baumann, who passionately sided with Zinner, and did not refrain from casting suspicion on Jhering and all other critics of this brilliant author. We learned that this Dr. Baumann was the family doctor of the Zinner-Erpenbecks, and when I took an excursion in the summer to the Scharmützelsee, Hedda Zinner's weekend house was pointed out to me, incidentally a real mansion. There were three names on the door: Zinner, Erpenbeck, Dr. Baumann.

It was not for this reason, however, that we decided against printing the letter, but rather because, after checking with Mückenberger and Boockh, we determined that it was unprofessional and would have given rise to embarrassing discussions. The CC organized instead a restrained letter from Dr. Manfred Häckel—but Frau Zinner said she was not satisfied, although the whole state of affairs was explained to her. She went around complaining to anyone who would listen, and she managed to get Ulbricht's ear; I assume this explains the repeated comment in Ulbricht's speeches that in *Sonntag* progressive opinions had not been allowed to be heard, but had rather been suppressed.

The Twentieth Party Congress

The Twentieth Party Congress gave us all a big surprise. The sudden stinging criticism of Stalin's mistakes hit us like a blow to the head. From the Western press we learned that in addition to the published speech there was also supposed to have been a speech by Khrushchev at a secret meeting in which he ruthlessly laid bare Stalin's crimes—there was no longer any talk of mistakes.

Eagerly we awaited the report of the German delegation. With his characteristic lack of subtlety Ulbricht explained in his article that Stalin was no classic, and he charged the younger generation with having been too preoccupied with Stalin. I believe he never received such an indignant reaction.

We organized several Party meetings during this time, and when I think back on it now, it seems to me that we had never discussed the Party's policies so seriously and responsibly. The Third Party Conference of the SED could not satisfy us, since hardly anything worth mentioning was said about the burning problems of the moment. It was more a conference on the economic aspects of the plan. Thus every discussion of the Twentieth Party Congress involved criticism of the way we had interpreted it.

It was in these discussions that my close relationship with Janka and Harich actually began. We could not reconcile ourselves to making Stalin the scapegoat for everything terrible that had happened. Blaming the cult of personality for undesirable developments seemed to us inadequate, idealistic. The official announcement said: Mistakes have been made; Stalin bears the brunt of the responsibility; that is now over. To us it seemed sheer effrontery to characterize the murder and other sorts of punishment of thousands of innocent Communists as "mistakes." And besides, what had made such distortions of socialist humaneness, of socialism in general possible? What was the economic and political basis for them? The Party leadership remained silent; they even made it known more than once that such considerations were inappropriate, that we should look to the future and so on. Yes, it's easy for them to say: Don't talk about the mistakes of the past; seize control of the future! How can a Marxist embark on a new path without having thoroughly analyzed what has gone before, without being completely clear about what is happening in the world!

That intellectuals in particular showed such a strong interest in the theoretical side of the new policies was no surprise. I do not know what was said about the Twentieth Party Congress in workers' circles. If the new questions did not cause quite a stir there, that speaks badly for our past work in political education.

Among the writers discussion raged, if also with a certain lack of direction. I remember the first Party meeting of the Berlin writers. In his talk, Helmut Schlemm from the Culture Department avoided all questions that dealt with Stalin's fall from grace. Those who were impatient to know more about it he advised not to be such sensation-seekers, which aroused general protest.

At the next gathering KuBa summarized from memory information in the secret report. Those assembled did not show their excitement outwardly, but it stirred them deeply. The whole report, as afterwards in all low-level Party organizations, had more the character of a moral condemnation of Stalin, not of a principled critique of the Party's policies of the past, present, and future.

At this gathering Bodo Uhse took the podium, seeming extremely worked up, and said something along the lines of:

"Pretty soon they are going to say to us writers: 'Open your desk drawers!' and we'll open them, and there will be nothing in them."

In Poland, so we heard, Khrushchev's secret speech had been published—while here it was given orally in increasingly watered-down versions to the comrades and thereby essentially hushed up. The Western press saw to it that it was nevertheless published, and there was no one, I believe, among the intellectuals, at least in Berlin, who had not read it . . .

So the peculiar situation arose that the Twentieth Party Congress, which was considered by the Soviet Communist Party itself to be the most meaningful event since the October Revolution and to contain a wealth of possibilities for a true renaissance of the socialist movement, never really came to anything in the GDR. I had the opportunity to read the Czechoslovak and Polish press, and I was green with envy. With what boldness the journalists there brought up new questions, having left behind the arid pasture of desiccated dogma. Our Polish comrades were ahead of the pack; without a doubt history will one day recognize their accomplishments.

With great interest we pounced upon an article published in the form of an interview by Palmiro Togliatti in *Nuovi Argumenti*. Our papers reprinted it heavily edited, robbed of its key ideas, but *Freies Volk*—where official directives must not have worked—published i t word for word. Togliatti tried to analyze the cult of personality from a Marxist perspective; he believed that a whole system of faulty attitudes and actions had to be overcome. He also alluded to the thesis of multiple centers in the Communist movement.[*] He received a sharp rebuke from *Pravda*, however, and we never heard anything about his developing his thoughts further.

In the spring the Czechoslovak writers convened. We did not have the opportunity to send our own delegate, so we asked Max Zimmering for a report, which he then provided. On Thursday, the day it was published, Schlemm called me all excited, asking what we thought we were doing, printing such a report. Becher called me at home on Friday to tell me how marvelous he found Zimmering's report. I responded that other comrades had reacted differently.

---

[*]Togliatti, secretary-general of the Italian Communist Party, coined the term "polycentrism" to explain this concept. Polycentrism means having multiple centers of communism not controlled solely by Moscow.—Tr.

Whereupon Becher said: "Who was it? I'll speak to him!" He did, with the result that after Monday he also found the article offensive. Well, well, Becher—there was no relying on him during this period, torn between duty and desire . . .*

Impressions from the Czechoslovak Writers' Congress
Pravda vitezí! Truth conquers!

by Max Zimmering
(excerpt)
. . . He who goes as a guest to a congress that is supposed to last over a week and be conducted in a language he has not mastered does not exactly expect to be entertained. Still, you shouldn't count your chickens before they hatch—and also not count them out. The 2nd Congress of Czechoslovak Writers proved to be an extraordinarily exciting event, in which not only the approximately two hundred fifty assembled lyricists, novelists, dramatists, critics, and representatives of other areas of Czech and Slovak literature took a lively part, but in which literally the whole country participated. Literární Noviny, the writers' weekly newsletter, was in short supply in Prague because under the congress's motto of "In the name of Truth, Life, and Beauty" the "poets" in the parliament building were not engaged in highly theoretical treatments of complicated questions of aesthetics (there were those, too, of course), but rather in passionate debates on life itself, on everything that passed over all countries of the socialist camp as a cleansing spring storm, not without lightning and cloudbursts, but everywhere leaving the fresh green of healthy new growth. The writers of Czechoslovakia can consider themselves lucky that their congress provided topics for conversation in the street, on the bus, in factory cafeterias . . .

✳

Ninety-five keynote speeches, and from most of them resounded in various formulations the call and commitment to be the conscience of the people and not avoid the truth. Vasek Kána left

---

*"Pflicht und Neigung"—the notion espoused by Friedrich Schiller and others that humans should strive to achieve harmony between duty and desire.—Tr.

the strongest impression on me. We knew him from his play The
Karhan Brigade *and from the visit he had paid to our Republic a few
years ago. His contribution to the congress was free of any attempt
to shift the blame for negligence to others, was free of any attempt
to portray himself as a martyr for the suppressed truth. He warned
against striking out blindly because of bitterness and against
overstating the problems, driven more by feelings than reason. And
then followed his confession, simple, direct, without bathos and
without mercy:*

*"Today the day for self-criticism is here. We endeavor to
answer to our consciences. That is correct and necessary, because
otherwise we would be ashamed to look people in the face . . . We
cannot avoid responsibility, and I disagree with those who try to
deceive their consciences. They say: We have kept quiet because
we did not want to harm the cause of socialism; we prettied things
up in the belief that we were thereby helping to build socialism and
peace."*

Kána described this position as dishonest and continued:

*"Let us say it openly. We have kept quiet because we lacked
courage."*

*Demanding a public admission of failure from writers because
they were public figures, he exclaimed:*

*"I have shrunk back instead of fighting . . . I knew, for example,
that repressive measures against honest people did not serve the
cause of socialism and that instead they did damage to and
desecrated the ideas for which I have seen people give their lives
before my very eyes. I have seen people treated unjustly, their
worth as human beings assaulted, their minds underestimated, and
what have I done? Did I protest against it? No, I kept quiet, at times
tears came to my eyes, but only rarely did I stand up against it, only
rarely was I what I was supposed to be: the conscience of the
people. Factory workers are my closest friends. From their ranks I
came forth, to them I remain true, and above all to them I am also
accountable. I say that I was true to the workers, and today I must
ask myself: Did I always come to their aid when they needed me?
Did I protect them from the bureaucrats who dictated to them from
above, on the basis of purely theoretical calculations, absurd
production quotas? Did I defend them when they were materially
and morally persecuted for criticism? Did I protest when fully-
trained young apprentices went home at the end of the week with
half-empty pay envelopes? Did I always speak out for the*

innovators when they were treated unjustly? Did I defend the good sense of the factory people from the ignorance of the bureaucrats? Did I condemn the cadre system, which so often was based on mistrust of the people? Did I hit those puffed-up functionaries over the head when they barked at justifiably dissatisfied people? Did I publicly condemn the arrogance of the so-called higher cadres? Did I cross swords with those 'organizers' who organized our lives for us so much that it was impossible to live? . . . Did I publicly protest against the phenomenon that we who are seeking the way to socialism have not found the way to human beings? That we have seen in them only a machine for the realization of production quotas?"

✻

Proceeding from the present literary discussion on Poland, but at the same time grasping the essence of the Czechoslovak situation (and also directing important thoughts at us), Leon Kruczkovski, who along with many other foreign writers attended the congress, said the following:

"We (the writers) have suffered the most under the crippling effects of dogma; we have been particularly affected by the attempts to create a paltry critical mode under the rubric of a pseudo-Marxist aesthetic, and it is precisely in our work that all the bureaucratic monstrosities and administrative tendencies in the areas of art and literature have manifested themselves so horrendously . . ."

—Sonntag, 20 May 1957

16 February 1957 In early summer the Culture Department of the CC invited the editors in chief from newspapers and magazines devoted to culture and politics to a meeting. The topic was reviving artistic controversy. Herbert Sandberg, editor in chief of *Bildende Kunst*, spoke for all of us when he said: One could not rid oneself of the impression that the Party leadership did not wish new, probing discussion; the signal had to be given before the floodgates could open. On the contrary, said the comrades of the CC, we should feel free to begin the exchange of views. Did they really not understand that one cannot speak out on questions of art without rehashing the same old empty notions if at the same time or beforehand one cannot speak out just as freely on political and economic issues? Anything else is like trying to make an omelet without breaking eggs!

In the literature of our neighboring countries a new spirit was stirring—an intensified effort was being made to depict the inner contradictions of socialism. In Poland an excellent story by Brandys, "The Defense of Granada," was published, which received widespread attention in all the countries of our bloc. Our reader of Slavic manuscripts at Aufbau drew my attention to it—the same Düwel, by the way, who just a few weeks ago, on the day of my dismissal from the editorial staff, was one of the first to characterize the measure as correct! We had it translated and printed it in installments. In leading literary circles the story made a strong impression.

Nowa Kultura published some new poems by Adam Wazyk, which Wilhelm Tkaczyk then translated for us. We published two of them, together with new poems by Günter Kunert. They struck a new note in our literature, perhaps not yet mature and perfectly clear, but honest and passionate. I had a conversation about them with Willi Lewin, a colleague from the CC who voiced timid, touchy criticism of the poems. I argued forcefully against him because I found that our views on the unique possibilities of literature diverged widely. We parted with the following agreement: the CC would invite some comrade poets and literary scholars to a discussion of the poems, and if necessary, would arrange for a critical article against the poems. Despite my repeated reminders they, as often before, did not uphold the agreement—secretly letting their resentment against us smolder. I then recorded my view on the publication of such poems in the form of a "Dialogue on Poems."

Günter Kunert

The Voice

There suddenly blows a wind,
It smells fragrant and strong.
A voice utters words,
Unheard for so very long.

Lenin is dead for ever,
Yet we hear his sound.
The phonograph record with two cones of light,
Slowly goes round and round.

It is not a resurrection.
Only one night's work is done.
We went through a tunnel,
We and the Party, as one.

At the tunnel's end shine
The tracks like a machete.
Like the two rails
Are the Party and we.

Creeping together over icy peaks
And valleys of swampy land,
making for the horizon.
From the voice has come a command.

—*Sonntag*, 17 June 1956

Adam Wazyk

Dream of the Bureaucrats

In the land of fools,
centrally directed,
everyone toes the line in circles
just like clockwork.

The one at his desk
the other at his vise.
To each who putters along,
are assigned two guards.

The individual turnip
is tended by a civil servant.
The cost expended
equals the yield.

The steep pyramid
spews orders and titles.
A hail of stones,
a whirl of paperwork.

Those at the bottom are mistaken,
the head is infallible.
It shines in bronze,
wreathed in incense.

On the little pinhead
are five hundred angels,
they blow trumpets,
a very dry tone.

In the land of fools
the muse is paralyzed,
Yet she is nursed
by master clockmakers.

(Translated from the Polish into German by Wilhelm
Tkaczyk)

—*Sonntag*, 17 June 1956

Günter Kunert

While reason slumbers,
the monsters emerge
(On an etching by Goya)

There sits a man
His upper body slumped over the table, his head

Resting on the bed of his arms,
And sleeps.

Out of the gloomy background surge
Lemurs, battalions of shadowy
Bats, owls, ancient and malevolent
Their faces, flit around the sleeper.
Evil eyes, sharp claws, hard beaks.

Oh woe, if reason slumbers.

From the offices crawl spiders, blind and
Blistered white their eyes, they weave their webs
Around houses, doors, windows. In the water pipes
Dwell jellyfish, stretch their soft
Feelers through the rooms into the pots and
The mugs, full of curiosity, ice-cold,
On the street someone falls down. Were the
Chest cut open, you would find
The heart dried up, only nut-size,
Hard as wood.

On the corners dogs, their coats pink
In color, cigarettes between their worn teeth,
Wagging their tails. When the sun goes up and
Down, they wag their tails. Clouds, wind, and
Hail always greeted by the same
Tail-wagging.

Under the trees stands a painter, on
His shoulders black ravens, one hears
Them cawing, their sharp-pointed beaks
Aim for the poor man's eyes.

Over the musician's hands on the
Black and white keys scurry
Millipedes. The song they play
Is little disrupted by the musician's sounds,
And children sway in time,
Their legs brown and covered with bark, grown
In the earth with long toes as roots.

Oh woe, if reason awakens.

A man wakes up and stretches
His body and arms, raises
His head. The slumber has ended.
With a pen the awakened
Holds the monsters captive on paper.
They sink back into inessentiality,
The bats shrivel up, the owls
Lachrymose and featherless, fall to the ground, roll
Into the dark corners, where the shadows
Swallow them. The evil eyes shut
And the threatening
Beaks disintegrate like burned paper
That keeps its form until
a breath of air strikes it.

—*Sonntag*, 17 June 1956

Dialogue on Poems / *by GUSTAV JUST*

   Critic: What were you actually thinking of when you published a whole page of "New Verse" in Sonntag *No. 25?*
   Editor: What do you mean, didn't you like the poems?
   C: I didn't dislike all of them, but some of them I did. Less from the standpoint of form—Kunert and especially Wazyk are exceptional talents—but their message left me unsatisfied. Half-truths, distorted perspectives.
   E: A little more specific, please, more precise.
   C: Take for example Günter Kunert's poem "While Reason Slumbers . . ." The poet is meditating on one of Goya's etchings, but of course he's not interested in Goya's time, but in today. But what a biased view and depiction! Was reason slumbering when we disenfranchised the Junkers and transformed monopolies into people's property? Was reason slumbering when we began to establish the foundations of socialism?

E: But that's not at all what Kunert is writing about. Do you perhaps believe that Kunert denies or even disapproves of these democratic achievements of the last ten years?

C: That's not the question. Kunert's political attitude is above suspicion.

E. That is the first thing you should remember when you criticize his poems. And second: was and is reason always and everywhere awake in the past few years and today? Hasn't our soulless bureaucracy made difficulties for us, this antithesis of socialist-humanistic thought? Weren't there people who, as Kunert says: "Were the / chest cut open, you would find / the heart dried up, only nut-size, / hard as wood?"

C: Of course there were and are such phenomena. But they have a transitory character, and we're liquidating them; the writer must see and describe them from this perspective. Along with the dark he should also show the bright, and above all the path that leads from darkness into light.

E: Yet this optimism covers a wide range. It does not exclude periods of spiritual torment, just as a socialist society, as the Twentieth Party Congress clearly shows, is not free of individual and yes, even collective tragedy. Do you want to deny the poet who reacts as a sensitive seismograph to the anguish of his time, making himself a spokesman for these issues?

C: I don't want that. But don't you believe that people expect more from a poet? A solution, a way out, the answer?

E: Or in other words: the poet should write only about things he has come to terms with, things he has dealt with internally. The conflicts he experiences and expresses in his poems must be, from his personal viewpoint, past, left behind, resolved. That would mean essentially limiting the poet to illustrating what is already known, already solved.

C: So the poet may allow himself to present his readers with unfinished things, with half-truths?

E: But of course! That can't be avoided if he breaks new ground in theme, content, and technique. People have always rediscovered in the poetry of their time their own searching, their groping, that which was seething and fermenting in them. Instead of "half-truths" (by which you mean to say non-truth), you should say more clearly: a part of the truth. How could a single poet in a single work ever capture the whole truth! To expect that is to expect too much of literature.

C: Where does that leave the didactic role of art, its mission to shape political consciousness?

E: Don't view that too narrowly, don't restrict it to individual poems, and certainly not to this one alone! The relationship between the poet and his readers is not only that of giver and receiver, teacher and student, mentor and disciple. The reader does not just passively receive the ideas of the poet, but also contributes his own to what only in its totality is called literature.

C: But he can also, if we are so lenient, generate misconceptions, with harmful effects!

E: We mustn't be afraid of that. If you go into the forest, you cannot be afraid of wolves. If you reject schematicism, you cannot be afraid of making mistakes.

C: That seems very dangerous to me. How can you guarantee that in the end the correct view will triumph, issues will be dealt with and mistakes overcome?

E: By developing a genuine discourse, removing from the realm of literature all caviling, suspicion, intimidation, administrative meddling, by letting criticism finally fulfill its true purpose. You for example had objections to the poems published in No. 25. You should have written something immediately, in Sonntag *or somewhere else. Those with other opinions could have answered; perhaps even here or there a poet would have felt moved to express his reaction in a poem. With the exception of fascist or other hostile ideas we should publish all sorts of views, also in poems and other works of art—but then we should not receive them in silence, mutter about them in small circles or accusingly ask the editorial staff: How could you publish that? Rather we should speak openly, polemically, argumentatively about these things, or against, if that seems necessary.*

—*Sonntag*, 5 August 1956

16 February 1957 A little while later, near the end of June, the editors in chief of journals oriented towards the intelligentsia convened at Kurt Hager's, in a relaxed atmosphere. Hager disclosed to us that a plenary session of the CC would shortly look into the ideological questions raised by the Twentieth Party Congress—it was the 28th plenary session—and called upon us to at last take up the struggle between ideological viewpoints in our publications. I pointed out that our intellectuals had little desire to do that, that they had already been exhorted too often to engage in struggles of this nature, which had shortly thereafter been choked off again. The intellectuals were like a girl who has been stood up four times—she doesn't come the fifth time. Harich, editor in chief of the *Zeitschrift für Philosophie*, explained that every philosophic or theoretical discussion would inevitably lead to questions of basic political principles; so a beginning must be made by the key publication. In order to find a starting point for philosophic and artistic discussions, we would have to analyze the previous development of socialism from a Marxist perspective and place the issues raised by the so-called cult of personality on a materialist basis—there was no other way to do it.

Hager agreed with him in principle and promised that a circle of theoreticians and politicians would soon thoroughly discuss these problems, which was very satisfactory to all of us.

Had they really done it and not just promised to—as Ulbricht later promised Harich in a private conversation—everything would have turned out differently.

At this meeting Hager cited *Sonntag* as an example of criticism that overstepped advisable boundaries. He meant the publication of Adam Wazyk's poems, which were subversive. We could not reach agreement on this issue.

The 28th plenary session passed a resolution on ideological work that made us feel confident of our policy: confrontation without defamation of dissenters, creative courage to enter new areas. Things were moving along.

With Becher in Saarow

A week before this plenary session Becher invited us to his weekend house in Bad Saarow. The three of us went together, Janka, Zöger, and I, and I think we overwhelmed him somewhat. He was in an expansive mood and we drank an excellent Mosel wine.

Becher, as we gathered from what he said, had had a conversation with Ulbricht the day before that also dealt with *Sonntag*. Ulbricht must have leveled harsh criticism at us, but nothing more specific could be gotten out of Becher. Either he did not endorse this criticism, so that he was not ready to repeat it, or he had instructions to be friendly to us; there's no denying it—he was friendly. It was a frank exchange of views, in the course of which we were frequently in agreement. In such discussions Becher sat and always sits on the fence.

What he voiced as critical suggestions directed at us: We should raise the level of the paper by bringing in important writers more often, by acknowledging more often the successes and achievements of socialism, and in general by practicing constructive cultural policies. Ulbricht had said that there was only one newspaper that could get our cultural policy in shape, and that was *Sonntag*.

We were able to express whole-hearted agreement with all of these comments. In meetings of the editorial staff I had already been arguing for a long time that we should stop just yapping at official cultural policy, that we should publicly and ambitiously develop a constructive cultural policy, which, to be sure, would differ substantially from the one in force. But this plan was difficult, for without strong backing from the Cultural League and the active cooperation of leading artists and critics we could only grope our way forward. Here our Czech comrades had it easier: behind them stood their Writers' Union with all its muscle.

17 February 1957 We kept asking ourselves on the way home and also during the next few days: What did Becher want, or what was he instructed to want, from us? Beginning with the tone of the invitation and his sullen greeting in Saarow, everything had suggested that we should prepare ourselves for massive recriminations, but then nothing of the sort? Zöger believed it was the new way of giving instructions; they did not want to boss the comrades around as crudely. Becher would now be talking to all the institutions and people under him in turn. It is possible that Zöger was right.

Becher did cause us one disappointment. Our collars at *Sonntag* had been too tight for a long time already. The "Republic" project had been quietly buried, but the concept of it had survived: a paper for the intelligentsia. And that's what *Sonntag* was supposed to become. Previously a simple cultural daily, a smattering of art and literature—and now in addition it was supposed to speak to technical specialists. Science, technology, as well as domestic and foreign policy, all geared towards the intelligentsia. Our twelve pages in small format was not enough. We had in mind sixteen pages, in the format of Karl Marx's *Rheinische Zeitung*—we thought we could manage that with the staffing at our disposal. We had submitted the project to the executive council of the Cultural League in May and it had met with approval. The final decision was of course in the hands of the CC, and it came out negative. Thus Becher informed us during the conversation in Saarow that an expansion was out of the question, due to the paper shortage. From Hager we later learned that he and Wandel were supposed to talk to us about our position before any expansion. Yet this, too, never got beyond the intention. Were both of them really overworked? How much time did Wandel later spend on *Sonntag* alone when the crunch came? He could have saved himself a lot of trouble by acting sooner.

Abusch attacked us suddenly after the Young Artists' Congress. That should have made us suspicious, because we knew Abusch's keen nose always picked up changes in the weather. I did not take the affair too seriously because Anna Seghers had once said to me: "I've seen Abusch licking so many asses that it's become a medical problem!" Briefly stated, he was hurt that we had not printed his speech at the Young Artists' Congress verbatim. Because he did not want to state his reason publicly, he complained in an angry letter to Federal Secretary Kneschke that *Sonntag* did not have a proper cultural policy, that it oriented itself only towards Poland and China and thereby tried to create the impression that there was no clear-cut cultural policy in the GDR. The editorial staff created this impression primarily—and now the gun came out of its holster— by not printing the policy speeches of State Secretary Abusch.

The letter also met with unanimous disapproval in the Federal Secretariat; Kneschke was outraged at its tone and, as far as I know, put Abusch in his place. Abusch did not insist upon following up on all the issues he had touched on in his letter, but silently retracted it. But we had one more opponent in our ranks.

We all felt the need at that time to talk over these controversial issues in a knowledgeable circle. It is not true, as was later asserted, that we, especially I, wanted to ram our heads through the wall. Kneschke promised us such a discussion with Becher, Wandel, and Hager innumerable times, but it never came about.

We were all the more delighted when we learned in conversation with Brecht that he was completely on our side.

With Brecht in Buckow

I had made an appointment to see Brecht in Buckow during the last days of July. He was friendly on the telephone, as always: "You know, Just, that you can always come to me. I am looking forward to your visit," he said.

When Zöger learned of my planned visit, he asked me to take him along; he admired Brecht greatly, but had never met him personally. Thus three of us went; my wife came along.

When we reached the "Iron Villa," Brecht had not yet finished his midday nap. So we went down the path and swam in the splendid chalk-green waters of the Schermützelsee. As I write this, the enormity of the loss that Brecht's death means to us comes very strongly to mind. Had he lived, he would not have remained silent about certain recent events. With him alive, there would have been someone whom one could have asked for advice . . .

Brecht came to get us for tea, which we took in the gazebo. We had not seen each other for a long time, and he emphatically expressed his sympathy. Zöger he greeted somewhat reservedly. But because he was from *Sonntag* and I had brought him along, he was friendly to him as well.

In the gazebo a lively conversation ensued with Heli Weigel, with Jakob Walcher and his wife also present. I committed the inexcusable mistake of not immediately putting it down on paper, so I can write only what has stayed most clearly in my memory.

Brecht had high praise for *Sonntag*. He rebutted my objection that our circulation was not very high (only 40,000) with the comment that that was not the issue. The crucial thing was that such a newspaper with such a point of view existed at all in these times. He was especially fond of Wazyk's poems. He described him as the most significant poet between here and Beijing. He had decided to translate "Poem for Adults" and let us publish it; he hoped to be finished by September. When I mentioned some of the criticism of the Wazyk poems, he said we should not let ourselves be deterred by that. He offered us his support: if we wanted to publish poems of this kind again, he would write an introduction, shielding us with his authority.

When I asked whether he did not have new poems of his own for us, he answered with a roguish smile: he still had poems about the 17th of June, but they were too pointed, it was not yet the moment to publish them.

We talked a lot about the political situation and the process of democratization. He did not think very highly of the present Party leadership.

When I asked who else there was, he remarked that he could name fifteen capable people off the top of his head.

"There's a sailboat on the water," and he pointed to the lake, "which doesn't seem to want to move forward. And they set new sails, rebuild the keel, fiddle around with everything—but the real explanation is, there's no wind blowing! This is why socialism isn't moving along, because there is no wind blowing from below, because the workers are not pushing hard enough for socialism to be done right!"*

The issue preoccupied him quite a bit—we kept coming back to it. "They want to offer the workers more material goods and hope that that will make more wind blow. First fill your belly, then talk morality—to be sure, I wrote that, but not as my own belief, but as the point of view of the lumpenproletariat!"

We began talking about Yugoslavia; *Pravda* had just published an article by Kardely on the economic growth there. Brecht said he would like to go there. The Yugoslavs, it seemed to him, were following an admirable course. The workers' self-management was perhaps a development that would get the wind blowing again. We should not copy everything right away, that was in fact wrong. But we could still experiment, try things out, as in the theater. We could create various types of production facilities: some with full self-management, some with codetermination, and some with consultation, and then figure out what worked best.

When I complained that we were so few who came out publicly for new policies that we often felt like an island in the sea, he replied with a smile that there were sure to be many more such islands, and the islands would grow and grow, and one day the ocean would be covered over.

The conversation was lively, sometimes turbulent, and Brecht's eyes sparkled with pleasure and love of life. When Heli Weigel

---

*This metaphor also appears in the *Buckower Elegien*, a set of poems Brecht dedicated to the events of 17 June 1953. One verse goes: "If there were a wind / I could set a sail. / If there were no sail / I would make one out of sticks and plans." cf. Ilse Spittman and Karl Wilhelm Fricke, eds., *17. Juni 1953*, (Cologne: Verlag Wissenschaft und Politik, 1982), p. 92.—Tr.

asked him to think of his health and go and lie down again, he laughingly refused: He knew exactly what was good for him, and such conversations made him well. We separated with a long, cordial handshake. Who could have suspected that it would be the last time?

When I received word of Brecht's death on that black day in August, I was far from Berlin, in my old homeland in northern Bohemia, in the little house on the edge of the spruce forest in the Jizera Mountains. The thought immediately went through me: How we will miss this man, not only as a poet and playwright, but as a political figure . . .

Talks in Prague

18 February 1957   During my vacation, which we spent with dear relatives in our old homeland, we also made a two-day excursion to Prague. We were, as always, received warmly by our friends at *Literární noviny*. At night we met in the cozy wine cellar "U mecenáse" on Prague's Kleinseite; it was a harmonious, cheerful evening. Everyone was there: Ludvík Vesely, Sergei Machonin, even the editor in chief, Jan Pilár.

Naturally we also talked about what concerned us all: the new policy since the 20th Party Congress, the tremendous possibilities and prospects for a regeneration of intellectual life and all our social interactions. Brecht's death had also greatly disturbed our Czech friends. Thus I had to talk a lot about the poet, especially, of course, about our last conversation.

Then I also had to report on an important conversation that I had had in the last few days before going on vacation and almost overlooked just now in recapitulating events. Is it the early spring creeping like young wine into the blood that has made me so distracted?

Today is Monday. I spent Sunday with my parents-in-law in Durchwehna and came back here to Bad Schmiedeberg on foot. The trees were standing still as if holding their breath, but one sensed their surging energy, their lust to break out in a liberating scream. The air tasted cool, dry, and tart. The finches sang, and with an exasperating croaking crows swaggered over the green seedlings. And overhead stretched a pale blue sky, which shyly pulled wisps of clouds over its face. Spring is coming, winter must give way. I daydreamed as I went, wish-dreams: the Party leadership sees reason, the Soviet comrades join in, the opposition's program is discussed and of course approved by a Party majority, life in and outside the Party gets moving, it experiences a tremendous upswing, life in the GDR becomes more attractive, the fronts begin to shift, we break with the oppressive representatives of the old course, the leftist forces in the SPD mobilize and decisively expel their own representatives of the old course—which also, of course, exists over there, mutatis mutandis. That is the only path to an active unity, no, to unity of the working class and thereby reunification of Germany. Dreams—illusions?

July 1989 Today one may smile at such illusions. For they were illusions, above all illusions about what Khrushchev could realistically achieve. In the Soviet Union the time for such policies was not yet ripe. Today the Soviets are analyzing the reasons for Khrushchev's failure and the beginning of what is now called the period of stagnation. But don't dreams have their justification in politics? Don't the intellectuals in particular have to dream their pre-visions and hold on to them in the face of all the unpleasantness of reality?

When I reflect on my outlook at that time, there was so much emotion and naive belief in it, so little realistic appreciation of the real situation. We did not see ourselves that way at the time, felt convinced we were right, were enthusiastic about our own ideas, which we found echoed by many sympathizers in and outside the GDR.

18 February 1957 Another thing I reported to my friends in Prague was an unforgettable meeting with Georg Lukács. He spent his summer vacation in 1956 in the GDR. On his way to Schierke he stopped in Berlin for a few days. We had heard that Lilly Becher was supposed to accompany him and his wife to Schierke. At our request she expressed her readiness to persuade Lukács to write an article for *Sonntag* or give us a new piece of work for publication.

Then I had an opportunity to speak to Lukács himself in Berlin. Janka invited me to join him and Lukács for lunch in the Hotel Newa. I had seen Lukács for the first time at the Writers' Congress, but only from a distance. What particularly impressed me about him now were his politeness and unpretentious reserve.

We asked him above all for information on Hungary. Rákosi had just stepped down, Gerö had taken his place, a whole string of writers who had been disciplined in the springtime had come back into the Party. Rákosi's resignation had been forced because his position had become untenable, explained Lukács. Gerö was only a transitional figure; the process begun by the 20th Party Congress was unstoppable. The up-and-coming man in Hungary was Kádár, a younger comrade who had suffered sorely under Rákosi. We were astounded—we had never even heard this name. What about Imre Nagy, we wanted to know. Lukács spoke of him with little regard. He would probably have to be included, since he enjoyed a certain popularity in the country. But he was no powerful and significant figure.

July 1989 This appraisal of Nagy by Lukács did not prevent the latter from serving in Nagy's administration as a minister of culture, something which earned him persecution after the definitive failure of the people's uprising. It did not match Imre Nagy's tragic fate, but after his release from involuntary exile in Romania Lukács was shunned by the Kádár regime for many years. Only much later was he allowed to publish again. The mills of history grind slowly, but they grind—only a few days ago, after his political rehabilitation, Nagy was also legally rehabilitated by Hungary's Supreme Court. Around the same time János Kádár died, having been removed from every official post months earlier. Now as before, it is incomprehensible to me how a man tortured in Stalin's dungeons could, after coming to power himself, throw his own comrades into penal camps (like Tibor Déry and many others) or allow or order their execution, like that of Imre Nagy, Pal Maleter, and all the rest.

18 February 1957 Lukács showed a strong interest in the developments in Yugoslavia. He told us he firmly intended to go there soon, to study the problems on the spot. His wife, who took part in the meal, made no secret of her admiration for the Yugoslavs' course. Both used the term "Stalinism" as an expression for that which was now overcome once and for all.

We also asked Lukács about the discussions in the so-called "Petöfi Club,"* which we had read about in the Western papers. He said this was a group of young intellectuals within the framework of the Hungarian Communist Youth Organization who organized discussions on topics of general interest in the manner of our own youth fora. He had also spoken there once, as had other writers and politicians.

In conclusion, he encouraged us to continue on our path and not let ourselves be deterred. He displayed a cheerful optimism that sprang from his deep conviction that the replacement of bureaucratism by democracy would also take place in Hungary peacefully, without any upheaval. His article about certain conclusions to be drawn from the notion of peaceful coexistence was infused with this same optimism, an article which Aufbau, directed by that paragon of circumspection Bodo Uhse, published in its September issue in a remarkable fit of boldness.

This same optimism inspired our friends in Prague and us as well. The thaw, it seemed to us, had once and for all prevailed over the severe and killing frost, and all that was needed now was the sustained tranquil influence of the sun to bring the country to bloom and to fertility. In every country the exponents of the old course were lying low, Ulbricht was giving no more speeches and writing no more articles, and from Poland came reports of the conflict between the so-called Nadolino Group and the unstoppable ascendancy of Gomulka. In the editorial ranks we had unanimity without much discussion, and, to make a long story short, the Cultural League was happy with us; many intellectuals praised us as Brecht had. For example, when the previously mentioned executive commission met to confer on expanding *Sonntag*, Arnold Zweig excused himself on the pretext of his work overload, but made inquiries as to whether changes were planned in the editorial staff— he would come then, of course, to prevent them. A person who also spoke out frequently in praise of us was Lilly Becher and I cannot imagine that she would have done so in conflict with her husband's opinion.

---

*Named after Sándor Petöfi, the mid-19th century Hungarian lyricist and national hero.—Tr.

Sonntag in Early Fall

A few days after we had visited Brecht he wrote me a short letter. In it he expressed once more his satisfaction that we had published the Polish poems, "because thereby one of the half-dozen iron curtains between the individual people's republics, the USSR, and China was visibly raised. The fact that we are part of a new whole is so far only a slogan, far from becoming a real feeling. These anachronistic curtains are suffocating us. Could you not publish more and more in *Sonntag* about cultural life in our sister states?" And in a postscript: "We know so little about the discussions going on in China and practically nothing at all about Yugoslavia."

We did our best. On Brecht's authority we turned to Oto Bihalyi-Merin, who actually supplied us with a correspondent in Belgrade. I wrote a commentary on Becher's visit to Yugoslavia, Lilly Becher wrote an article on Yugoslav art for us, our correspondent Ivan Ivanyi reported on modern Yugoslav literature, and I commissioned additional articles on discussions in literary magazines there.

Because the Hungarian writers had been rehabilitated, we printed a short, very critical story by Tibor Déry, as well as a new play by Julius Hay. Andor Gabor's widow was in Berlin just then, and we received an article from her through Lilly Becher, which Julius Hay had published in the *Volksstimme*, the central organ of the Austrian Communist Party (the KPÖ); he offered an apt assessment of the dispute between some of the communist writers and Rákosi's old Party leadership. While I was taking the waters in Bad Wilsnack, Zöger accepted for publication a report on cultural policy in Poland as well as an article on the intellectual resolutions of our Hungarian comrades. We also made an attempt to get an assessment of the Chinese Party Congress just then taking place, with its thesis of the "Line of the Masses," which brought up new ideas consistent with our own deliberations.

With few exceptions, however, our local writers persisted in their paralyzed silence. From many personal conversations I knew that most of them were harboring thoughts similar to ours. But their uneasiness with phenomena that distorted socialism took the form not of action, but of resignation, of an escape into safe topics.

Hermlin was the first to express himself in a poem on his earlier Stalin poems. It was, I think, a good and proper poem. When we visited him one time, we found him in a bitter, resigned mood—he had no desire to do anything, and used the first pretext that came to mind to discontinue his journalistic cooperation with us; he had been recording his thoughts in the form of a diary for us. He felt he was getting no response from readers. We attributed that to his one-sided choice of themes—nothing but "Fascism in West Germany"—which many of our readers, who felt well informed on such matters, would not find intellectually stimulating. Why didn't he write about that which preoccupied our intellectuals and most certainly him as well; but he did not want to.

KuBa had gone into shock after Khrushchev's Stalin speech, which he as a privileged member of the CC knew in its entirety. On a visit to his apartment I found him raging, furious, despairing—determined to fight for radical change. He declared himself enthusiastic about recording his everyday critical thoughts and observations in a continuing series for us. He did not write a single line.

The younger ones showed more activity. Kunert wrote a few poems that will one day be considered some of his better ones. Armin Müller sent us a poem called "This Night," an attempt at an honest settling of accounts that one could not read without being moved. Criticism was directed too much against outside forces; he depicted himself as the innocent lamb, for which we reproached him in a letter. He was not prepared to change anything, however, so we published the poem along with our correspondence. A discussion ensued but was soon terminated by Zöger because he did not think much of the poem and was skeptical of the value of such discussions.

Armin Müller

This Night

Quiet are the
calls of the locomotives,
extinguished the cold
light of the moon,
which lay on the roofs
like a late frost.
This night,
which you awaited
in the tormented, comfortless

twilights, has arrived
like hope
in the cockles of a girl's heart.
It surges from our lips
and we approach one another,
exchanging kisses
as before.

This night, my love,
speaks to us with the voices
that cross each other over the roofs,
heard amid the gabled
timbering of the halls,
which are filled with music
and bashful whisperings.
This night,
warm like the shoulders
of one's dear one and trembling,
brings the forests to collapse
that luxuriated before the thresholds,
darkening the way for us
on the slopes of curiosity.
Voices flutter
through opened windows.
They beat like the wings
of swallows. You love these
birds, I know. They
take off, when the rain
dries up, from the recesses
of the roofs, and their feathers
sparkle like the children's
white letters.

Like the children's
white letters . . .
The song I wanted to
sing to them, when they
blossomed in the pillows
of our love, went
unsung.
The words I searched for

escaped me. Whispering
they hid themselves
in the distance, concealed
behind the lilac's foliage,
close with its perfume,
its overpowering sweetness.
Garlands of flowers obscured
the view for me. The wind,
fanning the branches,
brought with it the sounds
of summer, of security.
Only sometimes, in the
troubled dreams of the nights,
when the paper rustled before
my eyes and the bats
flitted through the darkness,
a word became audible,
a cooing, trembling,
solitary word.
It went around the lamp
like a drunken beetle
that singes its wings
in the sudden nearness
of electricity.
And in the morning,
with the opening of the newspaper
or on the way through the
gray, crumbling city,
this word came soaring
like the sail of a
cloud, like a snowflake
in March, or it flashed
in the mirrors of a car,
in the eyes
of a woman.

In the eyes of a woman . . .

Always, when the year
opened vistas of distant Atlantises,
in the airplanes and on

the podiums of gatherings,
your eyes were close by me,
warm and full of fear.
I wanted to honor and comfort
them, yet the pages
remained blank,
upon which the wax of the noisy
and quiet hours has dripped,
knocking like a knuckle.
I know you were waiting
for this word. My
lips searched for it
again and again,
yet . . .

Forgive me. The paths
that we take are
surrounded by the drums
of conflict. Fires burn
on every mountain, and the
living must know their way
in the heated, confused
strategy of these times.
It was necessary,
a thousand times necessary, to learn,
to differentiate from one another
the beating of the drumsticks,
not to be blind
before the flames, but
to search out those
that light the way for us,
yes, to be a torch oneself,
burning,
not tasting the soot
and the ashes, which fall on
the early blossoms, yes to be drum
and drumstick in one,
not shuddering before the pounding,
that suddenly smothers
the voice, one's own.

That suddenly smothers
the voice, one's own . . .
For the nights awakened
that remained without sleep
and without my word.
Uncertainty razed
with pain-giving sickle
verse after verse of mine.
Still on the lips, unspoken,
the words died
and fell down like the dead,
in the glow of the midday's
withered berries.
Laughter stumbled
out of the darkness of these
nights, the eyes discovered
the glittering play in others' eyes,
saw the balls dancing
in the hands of the practiced,
carrying off him
who is not accustomed
to catching with his hands
instead of with his
heart.

Instead
of with his heart . . .
Beating, twitching impatience,
thin is the wall
of satisfaction, thin,
much too thin.
Unspoken, yes,
unspeakable remained
that which bored into your back
the sudden knife.
In shock fell silent
inexperience,
searching for the lips
of the experienced. They, however,
did not move.

Did not move.

And the emptiness tormented,
surrounded by shoulders, shouted down
by words and calls.
You stood in the middle
and remained silent.

And now,
after the three hundred nights,
this one night . . .
The books open,
birds glide over the river
with tidings
of the resurrection.
The waters cleanse themselves
and shoulders feel one another
as before.

Under the eyelids
of this night awake
the unforgotten dreams.
We stir them with
the magic wand of our love.
The words ripen. Already I feel
its trembling, my love. And the
morning that announces itself
will be like the dew
on the grass,
like the gleam of a smile
on your face.

May 1956

—*Sonntag*, 8 July 1956

SONNTAG Editorial Office

Dear Herr Müller!
   We plan to publish your poem in our next issue, although, in our view, it manifests several weaknesses in contents, which we want briefly to set forth:
   Without a doubt everything you write is justified. Our criticism is therefore directed not at what you have written, but at what you have not written. Without doubt, a dialectical process has taken place in German literature in recent years—and not only there. Things would have been very simple if the pressure from the outside had encountered more or less massive resistance by the writers. But things were not that simple, unfortunately. This external pressure, expressed in the dogmatic interpretation of the particular function of writers, was matched by the willingness of the writers to submit to this pressure; one could call this attitude conformist. Only thus can it be explained that in these years, works appeared that conformed completely to these dogmatic requirements—yes, in regard to this dogmatism went one better. A criticism of the tendencies of the past years must therefore in our opinion call attention to this dialectic; in other words, the writer is obliged not only to practice criticism, but to also clarify his relationship to himself. Only in this way will criticism actually become productive. This clarification of one's relationship to oneself is missing from your poem. You put all the blame on influences from the outside, which might have the consequence that the public will view your poem not as criticism, but as an attempt to evade responsibility . . .

Armin Müller's Reply

Dear Colleagues,
   . . . You write: "Things would have been very simple if the pressure from the outside had encountered more or less massive resistance by the writers . . ." That is without doubt correct. Had I been speaking not of myself in my poem, but of the writers, your criticism would have been justified. But I am talking about myself. When I first stuck my nose into literature the dogmatists' roadsigns had already been put up. I came out of the past blind, experienced the changes hopefully, experienced them directly. I had no reason to doubt the usefulness of the roadsigns. I cooperated and was

firmly convinced I was serving the future with my verses. Where, I ask you, was this resistance you speak of supposed to come from?

Sometimes, admittedly, but only just recently, I have felt stifled, felt unhappy. For a long time I did not know why no more poetry came to me. Today I finally know . . .

I will stand behind what I believe. Should the poem give rise to a discussion, I would gladly say something further . . .

Editor's Note:

We are more than willing to provide space for a discussion of this poem and the accompanying correspondence.

—*Sonntag*, 5 August 1956

18 February 1957 We published a poem by Gerhard Zwerenz, "The Mother of Freedom is Called Revolution," a poem in our socialist spirit which, however, the bureaucrats misunderstood. I heard a few days ago that Zwerenz had to defend the poem in front of the Party in Leipzig.

Gerhard Zwerenz

The Mother of Freedom is Called Revolution

The old earth holds its breath,
heated gusts of revolution
again fill the halls.
The people shout for news,
Babies stare, astonished,
Beggars taste dreams of hope.

Failures plot revenge,
An arid one weeps manure water,
Windbags fly into a rage.
Life—shouts the crowd
and builds bridges into the here and now.
The epigones scream silently.

Life under the bell jar
of freedom breeds maggots,
which swarm in the closed container
and rot while still alive.

When the stove does not draw
you have the pipe cleaned
or a chimney built.
But you don't say a mass.

When earths suffer thirst
you water your flowers.
But you don't burn their
moisture-glowing faces.

When the revolution runs aground
and freedom seeps away
you wave with palms—
since when do lions sing psalms?

Lend your pen no one,
write for yourself,
let your flame burn down
except for the cry:
In the name of the revolution!
Do not squint,
look straight ahead;
where horizons arch,
looking into the night would be
a lie.
Do not talk, build,
do not flinch, go,
when your hand feels the compass,
let your mind raise anchor
from the muddy bottom
and the waves carry strength to you;
the rock beneath the lighthouse
raises itself sky-high!
Your goal draws you onward
and nothing more can delude you.

When the seagull circles mewing around the sail
I hear a warning
and wind fans my face,
so that the freshness remains
and eyelids do not droop in exhaustion.
Dull silence deceives
and brings sleep,
the boat lies quietly
yet sinking, because inertia
bores into it.

The revolution is not a nightcap,
in which one is gently bedded,
tassels tickling one's back.
Oceans are not puddles,
Sand, softly moistened,
to charm the boys.

But you've slept like boys,
for so long, only not so healthy.
The revolution ran aground,
and that in the middle of the harbor.

You slept the sleep of the unjust.
Awaken, and let us together
fight better!
The mother of freedom is called revolution.
Freedom is her daughter,
the Party her son.

—*Sonntag*, 1 July 1956

18 January 1957 His piece "Leipziger Allerlei"* caused even
more trouble for both him and us. We had commissioned him to
commit to paper some random observations about cultural life in
Leipzig, to touch on open questions, expose inconsistencies, in
short, to portray real life without preconceived views, and write an

---

*The name of a stew made with a hodgepodge of ingredients.—Tr.

article in the style that Brecht had recommended to me the past summer. Zwerenz wrote the piece, we published it. There was a scandal. It came to my attention because a few days beforehand I had complained to Lilly Becher that Wandel and the others showed a certain reserve, even dislike, toward *Sonntag*. She called me up: " I spoke with Com. Wandel yesterday about what he really had against you people. 'What do I have against them!' he said furiously, 'Read the article, then you'll know.' I read the article, Comrade Just, and it really isn't good." She meant "Leipziger Allerlei." At heart an article by a confirmed socialist. But if you took a sentence here and there out of context, a poisonous brew could be made out of it.

And then the furor in Leipzig! Siegfried Wagner saddled up his warhorse and led a furious charge against us, courageously supported by such sinister figures as the writer Kurt Houpt, whose literary activity for years now has consisted of writing a book with the support of stipends from the Writers' Union, but mainly serving as Party secretary of the Union's Leipzig branch. They concentrated their attack not on Zwerenz or *Sonntag* as a whole, but on me; Herzog's hand was clearly visible. I had written an article in the beginning of October against the "bitterly strict guardians of the Muses" in which I had gone on the warpath against further restrictions in Marxist aesthetics. A certain Henniger, secretary of the Cultural League in Leipzig, had now played his trump-card— countering this article with some passages from my little book from 1953 to demonstrate that I was unprincipled and inconsistent. I learned later that after my dismissal from the editorial staff he repeated this line of reasoning several times before Cultural League functionaries, so that he clearly earned his honorary title of "Arch-Foe of Just." We received an enormous amount of abuse from the Leipzig Stalinists in connection with "Leipziger Allerlei," and these fellows are certifiably entitled to the dubious renown of having uncovered our "counterrevolutionary activities" long before the Berliners did.

It speaks for the character and methods of these people that they themselves did not balk at libel; Karl Kneschke likewise spoke with me about the "Leipziger Allerlei"—he did not like the piece, which was his perfect right and was justified by several of Zwerenz's formulations. He also made it clear to me, however, that he did not approve of my article on the "guardians of the Muses." That made me think, because I respect Kneschke and value his opinion. He felt that the intellectuals in particular condemned the article because I had been a member of the CC and could not allow myself such a change in my thinking. When I asked which intellectuals he had in mind, he named Ernst Bloch and Hans Mayer, on the strength of information from regional secretary Henniger. The latter asserted at a closed meeting of the Leipzig Cultural League that Bloch, Mayer, and others would no longer participate in League projects because of my own and *Sonntag*'s position. A follow-up discussion between our editor Jochen Wenzel and Bloch and Mayer revealed the exact opposite: both thought *Sonntag* was on the right path and urged us to continue.

It would not be worth paying attention to this libel—if I had not been advised subsequently by well-intentioned friends to give in and not try to ram my head through a brick wall; after all, I might be mistaken. And I vacillated quite a bit, but I had only to remind myself of these methods, used not only by Henniger-types, to realize clearly that this could not be right.

All things considered, there was a lightning storm brewing over our heads, with only a spark needed to set it off.

July 1989 At our request, our independent contributor Jochen Wenzel from Leipzig, whom we wanted to recruit as an editor, participated in the activities of the Party and Cultural League in Leipzig as a representative of Sonntag *and reported on them in a memo that threw a telling light on prevailing conditions, on the thought processes and actions of many functionaries at the time.*

Autumn Storms

18 February 1957 In mid-October Wolfgang Joho reported to us on a meeting of the executive committee of the German Writers' Union. There had been heated discussions. Anna Seghers had left the meeting in a rage, slamming the door behind her. It concerned the secretary-general. Eduard Claudius had been picked for a position in the diplomatic service, and Max Zimmering had been chosen as his successor. The matter had been settled by a small group, without Anna Seghers, their president, who the day before the meeting had denied to Stefan Heym, in response to his inquiry, that there were any such plans, and now learned at the meeting that she had been misinformed.

Joho also reported on the strong dissatisfaction among writers in Berlin about the undemocratic way in which the directorate had been constituted at the congress at the beginning of the year. To make up for this defect, the executive committee had decided to convene a new delegates' conference sometime soon. We commissioned Joho to write a commentary on this imbroglio, which we condensed and made more pointed by calling upon writers to get involved, like their colleagues in the Soviet Union and the people's democracies who were supporting the process of democratization. The commentary was written ten days before the historic Eighth Plenary Session of the CC of the Polish United Workers' Party and appeared on the very day of the session, which gave it a thrust we admittedly did not intend. I don't think that his commentary "Writers and *res publica*" achieved much of an echo in intellectual circles, but in the CC it must have had an alarming effect all the way to the top.

Writers and res publica

Minds are on the move among us, as elsewhere. People are investigating, revising, criticizing, pondering, sorting out, striking balances, setting new goals. "People"—not just those who for professional reasons or out of inclination or need concern themselves with res publica, *that is, with public issues, and, like the man of the house, feel responsible for making sure that in the house of the Republic everything is in order. No, this time the movement has been much more far-reaching. It is even dawning on privacy fanatics that their jealously guarded private affairs cannot and will not remain untouched by changes in* res publica.

How much more movement must occur in the minds of those whose activity is very closely associated with the public, who, because they publish, must be included among the publicists (even when they claim the more prestigious title of "writer" for themselves). To them is entrusted not only to write about changes already underway, but also to play a part to assure that these changes move along the right path, that is, toward the correct goal. One hears from the Soviet Union and the people's democracies that there it is precisely the writers who have taken up with vehemence and passion the impulses emanating from the Twentieth Party Congress. It may be that one or the other may overshoot his mark, that from time to time an uninvited dissonant voice may be heard in the choir of those concerned with socialism—we are convinced that the writers themselves will take care of such phenomena.

But where are the opinions of the German writers in newspapers, magazines, assemblies—in short, in public? Occasionally a poem ventures forth that, more or less artistically, more or less courageously, touches upon crucial issues. Articles, essays, short stories, editorials? You can count them on the fingers of one hand. Otherwise silence in the forest, especially in the forest of leaflets. A creative restlessness has seized hold of our people, they sense the vibrations of the Twentieth Party Congress, in whose aftermath socialism is being purged of all unworthy distortions and is radiating an intensely magnified appeal. Is it worthy for a writer to let these turbulent developments rage all around him, about which he perhaps, when the storm-clouds have passed over and everything is resolved, means to write a story or novel? A writer here knows where people are being tweaked, he knows, as a recent exchange of views between several writers and the Politburo revealed, a wealth of questions to which our population expects answers.

We by no means want to restrict writers to expressing themselves on artistic and literary problems. With all due respect to art, aesthetics, and philosophy, questions of our political and social life are incomparably more important, questions on which we are interested in writers' opinions. It was they, for example, who could support a democratization initiated by the party of the working class and the National Front. But what, for example, is the writers' position on democratization in their own house, that is, in their union? They have a directorate whose election did not take place very democratically at the Writers' Congress. Are they keeping quiet about that? It would not be quite right to answer in the affirmative. They're getting angry, they're swearing, mutinying, criticizing—to be sure, only when among their own kind, in the Union. They cause a tempest, but, unfortunately, only in a teapot!

People expect, not unjustifiably and on the basis of historical examples, that where public issues are concerned a writer will sit in the front row as the conscience of his era and not disappear into his union, club, or coffee house to say clever and courageous things in private, or even close the shutters of his little house in the woods where, ears deaf to the gales, he works secretly on what the public needs today, not the day after tomorrow.

—*Sonntag*, 28 October 1956

18 February 1957 On Sunday, I think it was 23 October, we learned, unfortunately not through our press, about the momentous changes in Poland. Gomulka's speech at the Eighth Plenary Session, which I heard on a western radio station and later read in the *Frankfurter Allgemeine* and the Wroclaw *Arbeiterstimme*, made a deep and lasting impression on me. That had a new sound, that was the truth! A world away from the standardized, cliché-ridden sermons to which we had been treated in recent years. In Poland forces with which we felt a strong bond had triumphed.

We were not fully unprepared for what took place during "The Five Days That Shook Poland." Polish writers and journalists had visited us many times. Only a few days before the plenary session Roman Karst had reported on Poland to the board of directors of the German Writers' Union; Joho had told us about it. Our writers, however, were not prepared to follow their Polish colleagues; that would be going too far for them and seemed too bold. (At the end of January I read an article by Roman Karst in a Polish magazine in which he expressed great bitterness over this encounter with his colleagues from Berlin.)

We met, pleasantly excited, on Monday in the editorial offices. Everyone was enthusiastic about the little bit of Gomulka's speech that had become public. Greedily we fell upon *Neues Deutschland*—nothing. On Tuesday nothing but a few wry comments. Good God, what's going on? The Monday edition of *BZ am Abend*, which had published parts of Gomulka's speech, was confiscated! One could not rid oneself of the impression that our Party leadership was viewing the developments in Poland with extreme suspicion and displeasure. But why? Who could not grasp that something of incalculable significance for the entire international workers' movement was taking place in Poland? The replacement of Stalinism by genuine communism! A new era was dawning, an era of truth, of humane socialism.

Our hearts beat with love and solidarity for our Polish comrades, but how could we tell them? The daily papers behaved abominably. They limited themselves to commenting on Adenauer's commentary on the events in Poland. They thereby gave the impression to the average consumers of state propaganda that actually very disturbing things were happening in Poland, things whose outcome could not be predicted. Fat Siggi Wagner, the cultural boss and arch-Stalinist in Leipzig, spoke out along these lines: "The misfortune of the

Polish people lies in the sudden death of Boleslav Bierut, because he had the Party and state under control and was loved by the Polish people. Now things hostile to the Party are coming out of Poland, but our path is independent of Poland's . . ."

We held a short Party meeting on this same day at which all the comrades expressed their indignation at the one-sided, inadequate information on Poland and delegated the Party secretary to ask for an appointment with the regional leadership to discuss the matter.

On Tuesday evening Harich, Zöger, and I went to the Polish embassy to obtain information on Poland from the cultural attaché, Mrs. Jakubovska. Distressed and dismayed at the conduct of the German press and Party leadership, she was all the more delighted at our visit, although she displayed the required diplomatic restraint, and gave us *Trybuna Ludu* with Gomulka's speech in it. She must have thought to herself: What cowards, these guys from *Sonntag*; they declare their sympathy with developments in Poland, but do not dare to write that in their paper . . . She was right, a thousand times over. We all buckled under. I know that there were comrades in every editorial staff whose hearts were filled like ours with ardent sympathy for Poland, for Gomulka, yet no one stepped out of line . . .

To do justice to the truth, I must record that we made an attempt. After long discussions on Tuesday Harich had written a commentary on Poland that we had to reject because it was excessive. I myself sat down that evening and wrote a carefully balanced commentary, in which I set forth the progressive and fundamentally socialist character of this Polish October, moreover pointing out that the Polish working class, in following this new path, accompanied by our sympathies, would gather experiences important for all parties. In conclusion I criticized the conduct of the dailies, which should have been reporting regularly on Poland.

I do not want to assert that we thereby saved the honor of the German socialist press, but we nevertheless were the only ones on that Thursday to sound such notes, and this little article was used to beat me over the head when the time came to settle accounts.

Truth and Speculation

In Warsaw this past weekend the CC of the Polish United Workers'
Party met, elected a new Politburo and installed Wladyslaw

Gomulka as its First Secretary. In a policy speech distinguished by its ruthless candor, its undogmatic analysis of reality, and its spirited language free of jargon, Gomulka outlined his plans for the future. As indicated by the Polish press and radio, this meeting of the CC has caused tremendous stir among the masses. The workers, peasants, and intellectuals of the people's Poland are reaffirming in proclamations and resolutions their determination to pursue the building of socialism with new vigor, are rejecting all attempts to use present economic difficulties as propaganda against the cradle of the socialist revolution, the Soviet Union, and are declaring their confidence in the Party and its leadership.

Dulles, Adenauer, and various other exponents of hopeless backwardness have got these events all wrong. They're reveling in wild speculations about "the crumbling of the Eastern bloc," "Warsaw's renunciation of Moscow," and "the collapse of socialism in Poland." That these leaders are merely seeing what they want to see need hardly be said. These gentlemen are once bitten but not twice shy; they have no sense for the processes of history. While the wheels of history are turning forward, they cling to the notion that they can reverse social progress somewhere in the world. The zealous journalists in their entourage thus seize on every self-critical word heard in the Soviet Union and the people's democracies, especially since the Twentieth Party Congress of the Soviet Communist Party. Of course they are exploiting the above-mentioned speech by Gomulka, in the deluded hope of recasting it in their own terms. In their blind fervor they fail to notice that by doing this they refute their own main demagogic objection to socialism—the freedom of speech and thought it allegedly lacks.

"Go your own way and never mind what people say!" Marx once called this one of his favorite maxims. We are convinced that the Polish socialists will not let themselves be influenced or led astray by any provocative ranting or hypocritical expressions of sympathy. It will be interesting to see what noteworthy experiences the revolutionary workers' movement in Poland will gather on its new path.

In light of the above consideration it certainly seems odd that our dailies and radio stations have up to now failed to inform the population of our Republic fully and in detail on the Eighth Plenary Session of the CC of the Polish United Workers' Party and on current political discussions in our neighboring country. Our people would justifiably like to learn from our press and radio what course

*this important congress chose for the further development of
socialism, a course with which, in the words of* Trybuna Ludu, *a
"new chapter in postwar Polish history has begun."*

—G.J.

—*Sonntag*, 28 October 1956

*July 1989 How the behavior of our Party leadership and press—
on this issue in loyal alliance with the Soviet Union,
Czechoslovakia, Bulgaria, and the others—was received in Poland
is attested to in an article by the respected Polish journalist Edda
Werfel; I include this interesting document of our times here, as it
may well be largely unknown.**

18 February 1957 On Friday Zöger went on his long-planned
visit to Prague. We wanted to strengthen cooperation with our
friends in the press there. I had laid the groundwork during my
vacation. The plan to formulate new cultural policies could not be
realized without assurances of international cooperation. We thus
came up with the plan to arrange a meeting of the editors in chief of
Sonntag, Nowa Kultura, and *Literární noviny* in December to plan
further cooperation and coordinate the principles governing our
initiatives in the various arts. Pilár was very taken with this plan
and Zöger wanted to come to some concrete agreements with him.

Once again I almost forgot to mention something important.
When I delivered my commentary on Poland to the editorial offices
on Wednesday morning, Harich read it. He ungrudgingly thought it
better than his own, which he agreed to retract at once. As a
substitute, however, he had formulated a short anecdote we had told
him the day before. We had it from Joho, who had heard it from the
two Polish writers at the above-mentioned board meeting of the
German Writers' Union. Harich had formulated it very nicely, this
anecdote about the current multiplication table: 2 x 2 = 9. It later
played an incriminating role against us—if those good people had
only known that Harich was the author! When he heard it, Ulbricht
supposedly said: "The arithmetic teacher, that's supposed to be me!"
In Leipzig, where today 2 x 2 again equals 9, if not 10, they were
equally livid. Becher, however, liked it very much at the time and

* This article appears in the appendix of the German version only.—Tr.

immediately worked it into his own writing. That's no joke! A few days later Janka told me, in fact, that Becher was sending him in installments the manuscript for the new edition of his *Poetic Confession*. And included was an observation along the following lines: just read an anecdote . . . very apropos for many of our people . . . Becher never owned up to this in my presence, and I never made use of the information. Ernst Bloch at any rate considered this 2 x 2 is 9 the best contribution that *Sonntag* or any other paper had published in years.

A Current Multiplication Table

In the school in Schilda* the children were for many years taught the equation:

$$2 \times 2 = 9$$

One day this came out, and the teaching staff convened at a special meeting, at which they debated how to remedy this embarrassing situation. What had to be avoided above all was any threat to the authority of the experienced and indispensable math teacher. Also, the youths' capacity to comprehend should not be suddenly overwhelmed. With this in mind, the colleagues resolved on the basis of their extensive pedagogic experience not to hit the students with the unfamiliar truth in one fell swoop, but to introduce it to them cautiously, little by little. The math teacher thus received instructions to clarify first that 2 x 2 did not, as before, equal 9, but 8. On each succeeding day he was supposed to reduce the product by one, until finally the real product of the multiplication in question would be reached. But this cleverly devised plan did not come off. It failed because of the precociousness of the unruly children. On the second day, when they were supposed to be seduced into believing that 2 x 2 did not equal 8 but 7, during recess they had already secretly scribbled up the walls of the bathroom with the equation:

$$2 \times 2 = 4.$$

---

*A mythical town in German folklore whose citizens are known for their foolish pranks.—Tr.

The rumor that members of the teaching staff subsequently voiced regret at the abolition of corporal punishment is a libel lacking any basis in fact.

4 March 1957 Back in Bad Schmiedeberg. The people are in the streets drunkenly celebrating the Monday before Lent, bawling out imported carnival songs and enjoying, if somewhat hesitantly, the traditional freedom to kiss all and sundry.

I am working on my book again and have much to add. I'm in no mood for Fasching. We're still waiting for the trial of the Harich Circle to begin. The Harich Circle—I always thought it was some group of obscure people whom Harich had assembled in a childish fit of playing armchair politics. But the Central Party Control Commission set me straight. On 26 February I received a letter from the main office of the CC inviting me to a "discussion" at the regional administrative headquarters. I found myself facing three comrades: Herta Geffke, Sens, and Eichholz (Regional Party Control Commission, Berlin). They began the "discussion" as follows: "The Politburo has ordered us to institute Party proceedings against you as a member of Harich's subversive circle."

Then I knew what hour had struck. So we were the Harich Circle, the comrades from *Sonntag*, from Aufbau, and the academic institutes with which Harich had been involved. Everything that Ulbricht had said at the 30th plenary session was supposed to apply to us. It does not apply, therefore he must have lied.

They had prepared questions for me, which I could see on a piece of paper Herta Geffke had before her. They were similar to the questions used at the interrogation by the State Security, which I shall discuss later. The Stasi's cooperation with the Party leadership seems to be working splendidly, for in his questions for me Sens kept using transcripts of Harich's testimony.

Once again it was about Harich's and our concept, about our platform. I stated emphatically that neither a Harich circle nor a platform of any such group was known to me. I agreed with many of Harich's views, disagreed with some, but had never considered him my leader. "That doesn't mean anything," Sens said, "maybe you were the leader!"

The whole procedure boiled down to the charge that we had formed a subversive factional group. Proceedings like these are being carried out against everyone who knew Harich's views: Zöger, Schubert, Caspar, Düwel, Alfred Kosing—those are the ones I know about. Punishment will be based on how each individual behaved after Harich's arrest and today. I count on being expelled from the Party.

I would be lying if I said that this prospect does not depress me. But come what may: I feel strongly that I am right, am convinced that I represent the new wave of developments. It is difficult to maintain this belief when everyone is caving in, kowtowing, falling in line, leaving me out in the rain. Many people know me, after all. When they hear derogatory things about me, why don't they feel a desire to come to talk to me directly? But nobody approaches me. It's as though I've been written off, put on ice. But I will not knuckle under.

We Receive A Censor

Infected by the Polish example, Hungarian workers and students had also taken to the streets. Imre Nagy had overnight become the prime minister, with Lukács in his cabinet as Minister of Culture, while Gerö, that loyal follower of Rákosi, had railed at the peacefully demonstrating masses and called in Soviet tanks. Shooting and street-fighting resulted. Of course the ever-ready reactionaries seized this opportunity to go on the offensive. Hungary was setting out on an ill-omened path.

At first we did not receive any reports. The Party leadership did not take a position. Gerö had to give way to Kádár, but it all came too late and under pressure from below. We were all groping in the dark. Every day we huddled together, Harich, Janka, Schubert, the editorial staff, whoever came by. What was there to do? How were we to judge the course of events? Lukács was a minister, which offered us some guarantee. On the other hand, what about his opinion of Nagy expressed just this past summer? One thing at any rate was clear, and repeatedly formulated by Janka: a Party could not postpone necessary changes, could not let itself be squeezed by the desperate masses. Once a cart has begun rolling down a mountain, it is fearfully difficult, if not impossible, to change its course.

In an editorial staff meeting we came to the following conclusion: the Hungarian developments had taken such a disastrous course that great danger had arisen for everyone in our camp.

Therefore one should not write or do anything which, even unintentionally, could sow seeds of dissension. Therefore: extreme caution in editing the paper.

I was called to see Becher that same afternoon. He was overwrought, angry, irritable. I gathered from his words that he had had a confrontation with Ulbricht the day before. The comrades in the Politburo were extremely angry with *Sonntag*. The commentary "Writers und *res publica*" had annoyed them especially; it was a direct summons to the intellectuals to follow the Hungarian path and was thus a subversive article. Likewise "Leipziger Allerlei" and various other things—a sign that we did not understand our editorial responsibilities. Becher closed with the pronouncement that, as president of the Cultural League, he had decided to assign an adviser to us for the duration of these difficult and complicated developments: Klaus Gysi. He was waiting in the antechamber and was now brought in.

I offered my resignation. Becher became more reasonable, hastening to say that these measures were not directed against Zöger and me; Gysi was merely being assigned to us to help out; everyone understood that in such times editing a paper like *Sonntag* was a complicated matter.

We talked a while longer about Poland and Hungary. I had the impression that Gysi largely agreed with us. He seemed to approach his job of adviser reluctantly—after all we had always had a good relationship, based on mutual respect.

As we drove back together, Gysi admitted to me that the whole thing had taken a somewhat different course. According to him, Becher and Abusch had begged him for an hour to take over as editor in chief of *Sonntag*, and only when he refused to budge had they fallen back on the "adviser" solution.

My report of the conversation with Becher and the arrangement he had imposed aroused violent opposition among the editorial staff. Expressions such as "censor," "commissar," and "natschalnik"* were immediately heard. I calmed my colleagues, urging them to show understanding and discipline; from the short talk with Gysi I had the impression that he was reasonable, that we would be able to manage with him.

That afternoon Gysi introduced himself to the editorial staff, who in no way received him like a welcome guest. Harich had

*Russian for "boss," especially one who is a Party functionary.—Tr.

somehow learned of it, burst in suddenly and showered Gysi with reproaches for accepting such an assignment. Gysi defended himself by letting it be known that he thought exactly as we did.

Later in the day Paul Wiens brought us an article that was no longer "acceptable." I explained this to him and used the opportunity to inform him that at the moment Gysi had the final word. Later on Becher held this very much against me. But was Gysi's appointment supposed to be kept a secret? And was that even possible? The following day Wiens brought the matter up with the Berlin Writers' Union steering committee, and the impulsive Hedda Zinner had nothing better to do than report it to Becher while the news was red-hot.

Two days later I was invited to Becher's villa for dinner. We talked, at least from my side, very openly, and on this occasion Becher served up my alleged indiscretion to me. He showed me a poem he had written on Rajk's execution. Of course I wanted to have it immediately for *Sonntag*, but he furiously pointed out to me that one had to know what one could publish when. Did I believe that it had been easy for him to sit in the Hotel Lux with his bags packed, expecting to be arrested at any moment? He gave me some insignificant love poems instead, which we obediently printed.

That evening Becher assembled the Berlin writers' steering committee; he announced Gysi's appointment as a legal and thoroughly unsensational measure and urged people to keep a clear head.

The Party leadership had in the meantime taken a position on the events in Hungary. According to their account, the intellectuals of the Petőfi circle were really the culprits: through wild, negative discussions they had undermined trust in the people's government. Rákosi's errors and crimes were barely mentioned. No reasonable person agreed with this assessment, and even Becher commented that cause and effect were being reversed.

The objective of this line of argument was clear to me from the outset. The most prominent advocates of democratization in every Party were the Communist intellectuals. That the developments in Poland had taken the course they had was for the most part due to the firm, courageous stand of the writers and journalists. If Party leadership, like Rákosi and Gerő in Hungary, stubbornly opposes these aspirations and reacts conservatively—as is generally known, Rákosi was still expelling leading Communist writers from the Party in early 1956—annoyance and resentment build up, and the intellectuals, who are not practiced and experienced politicians, overshoot their mark and respond to errors with errors. That applies without doubt to several essays by Julius Hay and Tibor Déry. And whether Lukács acted very intelligently when he went along with Nagy and sought asylum in the Yugoslav embassy is also doubtful.

If one sees a moral in all this, one must also speak of and criticize the mistakes of the Hungarian intellectuals. But if one talks only about their mistakes and lays the chief burden of responsibility at their door, one distorts the truth.

As far as I know, only our Party argued with this striking one-sidedness. They want to prevent Ulbricht's mistakes from being discussed—so they keep quiet about Rákosi. They want to silence our dissenting intellectuals, to intimidate them—they therefore cast the "counterrevolutionary" activities of the Petőfi people in the worst possible light.

The day after my talk with Becher a similar argument took place, this time with Adam and Schlemm in the Culture Department of the CC. Strong criticism of "Leipziger Allerlei," but all in a friendly manner. Nevertheless, for the time being the individual pages of each edition were to be submitted to the CC before going to press. Obviously everyone from Becher and Wandel to Adam had come under fire from the top and received orders to bring *Sonntag* into line.

The next day a meeting with Wandel. To my surprise a polite, friendly conversation. Everything was in flux, so I should be content with a short discussion. He, Wandel, was not really narrow-minded, I knew that, didn't I. But the danger was great of a resurgence of forces for restoration; voices were being heard among the intellectuals that were tantamount to a call for reestablishing bourgeois democracy.

I reported that we ourselves had already considered this possibility and reached a conclusion. The Hungarian developments had created a new situation, which we, of course, would take into account. We parted, it seemed, on good terms.

Herzog censored the pages together with Schlemm; an excerpt from John Rees had to be dropped. Already their tone was harsher and non-conciliatory.

Thus editorial control was taken out of my hands, and it happened so bit by bit that everyone gradually got used to it.

The White Terror in Hungary

On the next day, the last Thursday in October, Wandel's office called me at home around noontime. He asked if we could still make changes to the current edition. No, I answered, it's already been printed. I was to stop delivery and get over there immediately. I had to leave untouched the crisp duck we were about to enjoy in celebration of my Thursday off and go to the CC. Gysi was already there and had talked over everything with Abusch and Wandel. They told me the Party had reports from Hungary that counterrevolutionary gangs were perpetrating a white terror there. Gysi was writing an article on the subject, admonishing and warning the intellectuals. What I thought was important was not in it, namely, that the Party should never drift so far from the masses of workers that they could stand idly by, watching the activities of the counterrevolutionaries. We decided to reprint the first run. The editorial staff did exemplary work, Janka and the other comrades joined in, and in the course of a short afternoon we lined up contributions from Seghers, Zweig, Bloch, Renn, Uhse, and others. Hermlin wrote a good article right there in the office. We published a day late, but right up to the moment, taking a decisive stand on the menacing developments in Hungary.

When the Soviet tanks rolled in that Sunday, Kádár proclaimed his government and Nagy was deposed, I suspected a connection between these events and the urgency with which the CC had pushed us toward this course of action. I later heard that Nagy's government had the white terror under control that weekend. Nagy believed, however, whether correctly or incorrectly I dare not decide, that the situation was such that Hungary's continued participation in the Warsaw Pact would not be accepted by the masses. Apparently he was striving for a status similar to Yugoslavia's. One cannot yet form a clear picture of what was really going on because Nagy has not had a chance to speak out. I was only surprised that Lukács, whose opinion of Nagy I have recorded, stuck by him and went into exile with him in Romania.

In any case, the intervention of Soviet troops in Hungary did great damage to Communism's international prestige, put the Communist parties in Western countries in dire straits and in no way solved the Hungarian problem. We talked and talked about this issue, which deeply affected all socialists at the time, and essentially reached the following conclusion:

Swift action had been necessary in Hungary because Nagy would probably not have succeeded in switching over to the Yugoslav model. The restoration in Hungary entailed unforeseeable consequences for the entire bloc. It would have been smarter to deploy combined troops from the Warsaw Pact states and refuse Soviet ones. Here, however, practical military considerations, which we do not fully understand, played a role. One thus has to consider the intervention of troops as a necessary, albeit unfortunate, measure. There is no reason to rejoice, but because at the moment our adversaries are beating their drums, one has to stand firmly behind this action by the Soviets.

July 1989   Everyone knows what happened next. Kádár dealt bloodily with everyone who had played any prominent role in the events. Nagy, Pal Maleter, and many others were executed; Tibor Déry and Julius Hay, like many others, were thrown into prison. Kádár nevertheless managed to gain a certain popularity as János-Bacsi ("Uncle John") and bring a moderate prosperity to the country with his so-called "goulash Communism." He was finally sacked a year ago. He recently died and is being given a state funeral, yet at the same time the events of 1956 and his role in them are being reevaluated, a process that is not yet over. I cannot predict to what extent our interpretation at the time will be confirmed. In any case the same thing happened in 1968 in Czechoslovakia. Once again Soviet troops marched in, this time in union with the other Warsaw Pact countries, to forestall an alleged counterrevolution. And once again one heard the same Stalinist arguments as in 1956 in Hungary. It's high time the historians told the politicians and people what really happened.

Our Hungarian Lessons

4 March 1957   Despite the Party leadership's assertions to the contrary, we made no great distinction between Rákosi and Ulbricht. Even if Rákosi did permit several errors that did not occur here, perhaps because of different circumstances, like our constant necessary competition with the West, his modus operandi, the way he approached things, resembled those of our Party secretary very closely. Both are functionaries of the dyed-in-the-wool Stalinist type.

We further believed that our masses' stance towards the leadership did not differ fundamentally from the Hungarians'. The difference is at best quantitative, not qualitative, as the 17th of June showed. To prevent events like those in Hungary, the Party must move ahead with democratization as quickly as possible, so as to remove any potential for an explosion of discontent. As in Poland, the Party must place itself at the forefront of a movement that exists objectively among the masses in socialist countries—not imported by enemies!—so that the enemy cannot, as in Hungary, take over the movement. Here Poland and Hungary are always lumped together, mentioned in the same breath, but that is completely wrong. It is Poland that is showing what must be done to avoid another Hungary.

In any case, Hungary also taught us that in a country where socialism has not really taken hold in the hearts and minds of the masses because of their earlier fascist past and the errors of the Stalinist past, one could not behave like the Hungarian writers. For under these circumstances any Bolshevist self-criticism, and especially that presented in dazzling literary form, will be viewed by many people as an attack on socialism itself and can thus have the effect—of course unintended—of undermining what is left of the state's authority.

Thus we realized that the Polish way was no longer open to us. Destabilizing discussions could not be conducted in public, clarification had to take place within the Party. That was our line: formulate our thoughts and present them at an important Party forum. In Harich's proposals, often formulated on the spur of the moment, there seemed to me to be so many things worth thinking about that I repeatedly asked him to put them down on paper. Harich set to work, but I never laid eyes on the finished product.

I was, of course, not so naive as to believe that *Einheit* would print the article. But in any case, so I thought, the article would be discussed, perhaps in a circle of theoreticians from various areas, and certainly with members of the Party leadership. As the author Harich would have to insist on hearing the reaction of the Politburo or the CC to his views.

Other plans, so-called operational plans or whatever else Ulbricht charged us with having when he spoke at the 30th plenary session, we never came up with. After the Hungarian development disintegrated into counterrevolutionary activities and the Soviet Union assumed its position towards the whole issue, it was perfectly clear to us that at the moment there was nothing else to do but think through these problems again and again and try to approach members of the Party leadership with our ideas. All the talk about a conspiracy and plan of action formulated by the Harich Circle is conjuring up monsters to distract people from the leadership's mistakes. In Harich Ulbricht has finally found his scapegoat.

July 1989   It was of course more than conjuring up monsters; it was their conscious intent to stamp dissenting opinions as criminal, as Stalinists have always done and continue to do. The groundwork for prosecuting us was thus laid, but in my naiveté I did not see that at the time. Since then such procedures have been repeated many times: in 1968 in Czechoslovakia and today in China. The pattern is always the same: guilty are not those in power who refuse to yield to the legitimate democratic demands of the masses, but the spokesmen for those demands, who are always branded as counterrevolutionaries or even Western agents, and neutralized.

Harich With Puschkin and Ulbricht

4 March 1957   Since the 20th Party Congress we had been convinced that a strong group in the Soviet leadership was pushing for a consistent course of democratization. Malenkov and Mikoyan were its primary representatives, we believed, and Khrushchev sympathized with them. We were convinced, and despite all my bitter experiences this conviction has not left me even today, that the Soviets would not support Ulbricht's course in the long run because it did not advance their cause or ours in Germany one bit. But how deeply we were deceiving ourselves, how strongly the Soviet Union supported Ulbricht's policies, we were soon to learn.

One morning Harich called us up, greatly excited—it was the middle of November. He had been summoned to meet that afternoon with Ambassador Puschkin. We found this splendid. Harich came to the office and we discussed with Janka what one could and should present to the Soviet ambassador. We saw it as a tremendous opportunity to bypass the usual Party channels and inform our Soviet comrades of some views which they would otherwise never hear.

In response to our astonished question as to how he came by the honor of being received by Puschkin, Harich informed us that he had been working with a special Soviet agency for years and maintained certain contacts with West German politicians on its behalf. He didn't make himself any clearer, and I assumed that it had something to do with Soviet intelligence, with which many editors of the *Tägliche Rundschau* were known to cooperate. Harich also told us that he was routinely visited by representatives of the intelligence agency, who had him report on all sort of things, including current political issues. The relationship was such that he could call a spade a spade. And he would also do that with the ambassador.

I have to say that Janka and I felt very ill at ease. How easily anyone who ventures into this thicket of espionage and counterespionage can be torn to shreds! It seemed to us that recently Harich had been babbling too much, sharing his thoughts with just about anyone, not choosing his words, not paying attention to his surroundings. If only we had warned him more urgently of the danger! Today I am of the opinion that he did several foolish things that November from which we could have and should have protected him.

Harich spent four hours with Puschkin. His report on their candid conversation was devastating. The ambassador had tried to convince him that the present policies of the SED were the only correct ones, that Ulbricht was the most able man in the German workers' movement east and west, and that one had to support him. Harich's ideas were mere intellectual speculation that found no echo among the masses because the latter stood firmly behind Ulbricht and the policies he represented. Harich could not determine whether the ambassador really thought this way or was speaking only in his official capacity.

I had no illusions that Ulbricht would not immediately hear from Puschkin about this conversation. And in fact, only a few days passed before Harich was summoned to the greatest living German leader of workers. The meeting lasted two hours and Harich by no means had time to state all his views. Ulbricht argued ferociously with him and tried to convince him of how wrong he was. Harich told me that a cloud of power and menace hung over the whole thing, with the result that he became alarmed and "let himself be convinced." Ulbricht had unmistakably warned him that the Party would not tolerate any intellectual experiments like those in Hungary. He hinted, to be sure, that he might fulfill Harich's desire to have a circle of theoreticians and Party leaders discuss

Harich's theoretical views. To us that at least seemed a notable outcome of their conversation.

Later on, after Harich's arrest, at a Politburo discussion with the leading writers Ulbricht accused them of having heard Harich's speeches and not reported them to the Party. He said that he had heard Harich only once, but had immediately understood that Harich was the enemy . . .

We settled in for a long, harsh winter. At *Sonntag* we were groping our way from one issue to the next. Confusion and dejection reigned among the editorial staff. We were attacked from every direction, especially from Leipzig. Kneschke wrote a blunt and forceful conclusion to "Leipziger Allerlei" that elicited a flood of indignant letters, each one of which we sent back. I tried to stay out of it. After his return from Prague, Zöger got furious about the arrangement with Gysi. He stormed over to the CC to complain to Wandel, but came back tamed and "converted."* Only later did I learn that at that discussion Wandel had inoculated him against me.

Around this time a gathering of Berlin writers took place at which Wandel spoke. I was unfortunately unable to attend, but Fühmann and Max Lehmann told me exactly what had transpired. Several writers criticized failings of the press, which was not, of course, directed solely at *Sonntag*. And what did Wandel give as his answer? "We can run our press only with the people we have, and they are still deficient. There is a young comrade right now, an editor at *Sonntag*, who wants to modernize socialism, believes the 20th Party Congress to be more important than the October Revolution. Spend a few minutes talking with him, however, and he begins to tell war stories; scratch a little below the surface and the fascist officer in him comes out . . ." This boundless infamy was aimed at me, which everyone understood.

But this calumny fulfilled its purpose. At a Party gathering held to prepare for the delegates' conference of the Writers' Union I was nominated as a delegate but rejected by 24 votes to 17. I began to notice how the Party hatchet men were closing in on me. I wanted to beat them to it and chuck the whole thing, but Janka strongly advised me not to. If you're going to be hanged, he often said, you shouldn't do the hangman's work for him. Harich sometimes said in

---

*"*Gewandelt*." The root verb *Wandeln* means to change or convert; a play on Paul Wandel's name.—Tr.

jest: Just they'll kick out, Janka also, and me they'll lock up. It's better that way because afterwards they'll at least have a couple of people to rehabilitate.

With Janka and Paul Merker on the Day of Atonement

Janka told us Paul Merker's story. I didn't know any details of the case, only the CC resolution in 1951 that had severely reprimanded him. I knew from hearsay that he was working in an HO somewhere in Brandenburg. At a discussion (I believe it was about the New Course), Fred Oelssner declared that we would soon be having a big trial, which apparently referred to Merker. But it never came about, at least not in public.

Merker did get his trial, however. In 1955 (thus long after Stalin's death and Beria's liquidation) he was sentenced in secret to eight years in the penitentiary. He was incarcerated in Brandenburg and no one heard what had happened to him—not even his wife was told the exact circumstances.

In the summer of 1956 these proceedings were repeated. The trial lasted barely half an hour. The same judges found Merker innocent. He was released, in terrible shape physically and mentally. He returned to his wife in Luckenwalde, where before his arrest he had run the cafeteria. First he was allowed to recuperate somewhat in a Party convalescent home in Bad Elster.

The 29th plenary session in July had declared the 1951 Merker resolution invalid and rehabilitated Dahlem—the 30th plenary session elected him to the CC—but only partial amends were made for the injustice inflicted upon Merker. It was conceded only that the criminal prosecution of him had been improper. They took their time in restoring to him his rights as a Party member. Janka and I felt there was no question that Merker belonged back in the CC. Harich had the idea that Merker could become a kind of German Gomulka, but Janka, who was the only one among us who knew Merker and was friends with him, was skeptical. Janka firmly believed that the time was not ripe for a change in the Party leadership. He did think that it should be enlarged by the addition of Merker, Dahlem, and one or two other well-liked workers' functionaries.

In any case one had to support Merker's return to political life. He had been taken out of the picture so quietly that his case barely caused a ripple among a small circle of functionaries. Those who were persecuted with him suffered terrible fates: Kurt Müller was supposed to be set up for a show trial, which did not, however, come off. Then he was given over to the NKVD and disappeared in the Soviet Union until 1956, when he resurfaced in West Germany with other freed war criminals(!). Leo Bauer met with the same fate. Lex Ende died in exile in a small village in Saxony. Kreikemeyer disappeared without a trace. But Ulbricht declared: Crimes like Beria's do not happen here, we don't have any rehabilitating to do!

July 1989   *This version of things is still being hawked, most recently by intellectuals such as Stephan Hermlin and Ruth Berghaus, who asserted on various occasions (Hermlin in a* Spiegel *interview, the director Berghaus in a broadcast on West German TV) that Stalinism stopped at the door of the GDR. One can only wait until this dark chapter in the GDR's history is illuminated by the truth. I and others cannot get access to the archives and documents, but the relentless uncovering of all of Stalin's crimes in the Soviet Union gives rise to the hope that one day the silence will also be broken here.*

4 March 1957   We thus decided to let Paul Merker write articles for *Sonntag*. Janka talked it over with him in Bad Elster, and Merker agreed. After he returned from taking the waters we wanted to arrange the details with him.

That was the end of November. I had established a personal relationship with Janka. He had visited us in October with his splendid wife Lotte; Zöger was there too. We scheduled a return visit with him for the Day of Atonement, when we did not have to work. He arranged it so that Merker, Zöger, and Harich also came. I drove both of them and Heide in the staff car to Kleinmachnow.

This "meeting" on the Day of Atonement later played a major role. It was manna from heaven for proving a "conspiracy" by the Harich Circle. Of course we talked almost exclusively about politics that night—what else could you expect with people like that! Harich talked a lot, interestingly as always. We debated, raised objections. He also reported on his meeting with Ulbricht. Merker listened attentively. After all, he had been cut off from Party life for a long time and was interested in learning what sort of discussions were going on among intellectual comrades. He made a strong impression on me with his humane, calm, and thoughtful manner. He expressed himself only very reservedly, but seemed nonetheless to share many of our opinions. He evaded questions on personal matters, and we did not press him.

His concluding opinion was: at the moment one cannot do anything that will threaten Party unity. He said we should reflect on all the issues more thoroughly and continue to try to present new ideas to the Party's governing bodies for consideration. This view coincided fully with ours.

We did not discuss the matter, but I believe that Janka's hopes matched mine: we expected the imminent full rehabilitation of Merker, that is, his readmittance into the CC. Then there would be a comrade in it who was receptive to new democratic ways of thinking, who could thus possibly submit a platform to the CC for deliberation, to whose formulation we could add our two bits.

One thing has become clear to me, now that Ulbricht is firing on us with his biggest gun of all: a vague mood of opposition had infiltrated much of the Party at that time. Particularly among Party intellectuals new ideas were sprouting up in the various fields of expertise (economics, agriculture, etc.), ideas that did not come to fruition because of the suppression of intellectual life, and that surely contained errors, but that amounted in essence to the creative application of Marxism-Leninism to the present in Germany. I believe it can be argued that we at the publishing house and *Sonntag* were farthest along in the comprehensive formulation of these theoretical realizations and their political consequences. Had an open and free discussion been allowed, we probably would have become a rallying point for these forces.

That is, as stated, my opinion today (March 1957). At the time we in no way believed ourselves to be so significant or important. We felt like searchers, seekers after the truth, and were happy in this role. We were thoroughly optimistic, felt that right was on our side, as was the future. We would not have dreamt of engaging in adventures or experiments. The spirit of the 20th Party Congress was on our side.

Tito had given a major speech in Pola which was printed only in ridiculous, unimportant excerpts here, but in its entirety in the *Frankfurter Allgemeine*. Tito simultaneously approved of and regretted the intervention of Soviet troops in Hungary. He put the primary blame on the Rákosi-Gerö regime. His most important conclusion was: it was time for the Stalinists in the Soviet leadership to understand that the old methods were no longer acceptable.

Now Tito does not pull something like that out of thin air. That summer he met in the Crimea with Khrushchev and others under mysterious circumstances. He must therefore know if differences of opinion on the consequences of democratization and de-Stalinization exist among the Soviet leaders. Officially the Soviet Union scathingly repudiated Tito's stance; the Chinese also got somewhat involved in this controversy, and since then relations with Yugoslavia are again very strained. Our "hard-liners" immediately fell upon Yugoslavia with such excessive Saxon zeal that I cannot imagine how the situation can be smoothed over.

Discussion with Becher

Becher had long ago declared his readiness to discuss the political situation with the Aufbau editorial staff. The event took place on a Thursday, and if I am not mistaken, it was right after the Day of Atonement, on 22 November.

Becher came with his adjutant Thümmler and his wife Lilly. It turned out to be a very interesting evening, no doubt for Becher as well. He was in the unfortunate position of agreeing with many of our views but nonetheless having to represent the official policy as a member of the CC.

Janka spoke very circumspectly and cogently on the situation of the workers and the role of their committees. Lilly Becher was enthusiastic. I said that it did not satisfy us as theoreticians that mistakes were constantly being admitted and corrective measures taken. It was a matter of uncovering the causes of recurring errors, of finding their common denominator. To me this seemed to be an improper relationship between the leaders and the masses. I didn't say it, but I thought it—dictatorship over the proletariat instead of dictatorship of the proletariat. With unconcealed indignation Zöger brought up several serious problems. Harich theorized very intelligently and convincingly on the international situation and goings-on in the socialist camp.

Becher must have noticed that gradually themes were coming up that belonged in another setting; we were of the same opinion. He suggested continuing the discussion begun by Harich at some other time in a larger group, to which we agreed wholeheartedly.

When Becher left he seemed very pleased with the course the evening had taken. Lilly was openly enthusiastic. We hoped to resume the discussion soon.

July 1989   That never came about. And with this evening ends the first part of the diary I wrote in February and March 1957 at my parents' in Schmiedeberg. I was still able to celebrate my mother's birthday on 4 March, then I was summoned by telegram to Berlin—I had been called to appear as a witness at Harich's trial. I therefore went home, went to the trial as a witness and ended up a defendant. Four years in the prisons of Berlin-Lichtenberg and Bautzen followed, about which I shall speak later. I went back to my diary in 1962, the second year after my return from imprisonment, although the events were not as fresh in my memory. Again I allow my diary to speak unaltered.

II

Harich's Arrest—The Two Minds of Johannes R. Becher

(Diaries 1962/1989)

19 July 1962 Ückeritz. Five years later! The same book, the same theme, the same man writing down his thoughts and experiences. The same man?

A day at the beach on the Baltic lies behind me: sand, sun, blue ocean, healthy, happy people. They tan their bodies and cool themselves off in the salty, clear water. They laugh and flirt, and they did the same thing in the summer years from 1957 to 1960. These summers were stolen from me. Four summers of my life were spent in Ulbricht's penitentiaries; four times, with a heart aching with desire, I experienced spring from behind bars. Four autumns and three long winters I could only dream about skiing. "Four years in the penitentiary" was the sentence passed down by the High Court, and this barbarous terror-inspired penalty was imposed on me for alleged membership in the so-called Harich Circle, for counterrevolutionary activities hostile to the state. They let me serve forty-five out of the forty-eight months, then released me on an amnesty from Herr Ulbricht. His kindnesses are even more unbearable than his abuse.

I have thus been free since 30 November 1960. In the meantime the diary lay well-hidden at my parents'. What if it had fallen into the hands of snoopers from the Stasi! Even after my dismissal I didn't dare to fetch it. How could I be sure that some night a couple of stone-faced guys wouldn't appear in my apartment, turn everything inside out, and haul me away? Now I dare to. Why is that?

A few days ago somebody told me a joke on the beach. The GDR is renamed ARG—the Anton Günther Republic: It's quittin' time!* Yes, somehow it's quitting time for the Stalinist regime. The Ulbricht era is ending. Much too late for my tastes. This man has done much too much damage to the workers' movement, the revolutionary Party, and Germany. Apparently even now he is secure on his throne as a dictator, feared and hated, surrounded by his loyal and unquestioning minions. But developments in the Communist camp itself have moved beyond the Ulbricht-types, and that he is still in power is an anachronism not easily understood.

The result of his policies: a ruined economy, a stagnating and backward agriculture, embittered workers, peasants, and intellectuals, lethargy and resignation among the population, passivity and unprincipled careerism in the Party, rejection of the system by the majority of the German people. He has the borders

---

*Anton Günther was a Bohemian dialect poet.—Tr.

guarded as no German border has ever been guarded before, he has had to build a wall with barbed wire through the middle of Berlin so that the people do not all run away from him. What else must happen before the Party's honest core group pulls itself together and says: This man and his henchmen have to go!

Sometimes I doubt if these people, corrupted and kept down for years, will find the strength to free themselves from this evil. Sometimes it seems that the Party's conscience, embodied in the lives sacrificed in the struggle to free the working classes, is dead, suffocated by the big rear-end of this man who clawed his way to the top. But somewhere in me lives the belief, not based on anything rational, that the hour will come when right, morality, and decency will triumph. And if it's going to happen, it must happen soon. That is why I stayed here after my release from prison and did not go to the other Germany. That is why I have retrieved my diary and am continuing my notes.

No simple undertaking. I want to capture truthfully and without embellishment how I experienced the period in question. But people see their own past through the prism of their present outlook. And mine has changed a lot compared to 1956-7. Hohenschönhausen, Lichtenberg, Bautzen—they were my universities. The earlier Just seems like a naive schoolboy to me. But he wasn't, of course. He did a lot of good and made a lot of mistakes, but he always followed his true convictions without second thoughts about reward or punishment. I must avoid the danger of projecting present-day realizations onto my actions at the time. We indulged in a lot of illusions but our perspective was correct. Maybe we were too early with some things, but there always have to be people like that.

July 1989 *As these diary notes show, I hadn't changed much in this respect. My assessment of conditions and perspectives was correct, but my hopes did not take into account the long period of time such changes require. Ulbricht stayed in the saddle for a long time, and his followers continued his policies, cum grano salis. Essentially nothing has changed in the SED's policies, yet the GDR has not collapsed. And still—today more so than ever—the objective necessity of carrying out radical reforms is at hand. In the meantime, the motherland of socialism, the Soviet Union, is following this course. And there they call the long years after the 20th Party Congress the period of stagnation. When will the time come when people judge the Ulbricht and Honecker eras this harshly? Sometimes I doubt I will ever live to see it.*

The Premiere of Brecht's *Days of the Commune*

20 July 1962 As a representative of the editorial staff I went to Karl-Marx-Stadt the weekend after our evening with Becher; Brecht's *Days of the Commune* was premiering there. A mediocre performance and not Brecht's strongest play. There is something unfinished, something fragmentary about it.

After the performance there was a reception for which a whole bunch of Berlin intellectuals turned up. There were also guests from other countries. Janka and I sat for quite a while at a table with the Austrian comrade Bruno Frei. Frei thought as we did, and, according to him, so did the majority of Party intellectuals in Austria. Frei was optimistic. He believed that the Soviet Union was on the verge of a major rapprochement with the USA, that the international détente shaping up would create a climate favorable to further progression toward liberalization in the socialist camp. He himself, however, intended to go to China as a correspondent. We viewed that as an attempt to evade the confrontations pending in his own country and chided him for it. He openly admitted it, but apparently had more experience with the practices of Stalinists grimly defending their power—he went to China, whereas we ended up in jail . . .

I had a fairly lengthy conversation that same night with Alfred Kurella, who later rose in the Party leadership, and as "Kulturella" and "culture czar" carried out Ulbricht's cultural policies. Kurella was apparently intent on keeping up our long-standing and cordial relationship. "I know," he said, "that you people think I'm a Stalinist, but you're wrong. I'm just as interested as you in seeing that the mistakes of the past are overcome. You people go too far, however, just like our comrade writers in Poland and Hungary." A long argument ensued. I rather liked him. When he had returned from exile in Moscow in 1954 (why so late, I never understood), I was secretary of the Writers' Union and worked with him a good deal. He was well-read and educated, yet liked to act the superior comrade with experience in the Soviet Union. In the fall of 1956 he was director of the Institute for Literature in Leipzig, in whose founding I had participated. At the time Kurella was being driven into such a corner by the students there, among them Loest, Gloger, Brock, and others, that, in reference to Walter Ulbricht, he said that he, too, couldn't stand his voice and language . . . Which did not prevent Kurella later on from cozying up to Ulbricht.

Kurella urged me that same evening to visit his institute and stay with him. Abusch later joined the conversation. He was also for reforms, but he thought we were going too far and too fast.

I later learned from Janka that he had also spoken with Kurella that night. The latter had expressed his views in a manner characteristic of his outlook. As is generally known, his brother Heinrich Kurella, also an early Communist, fell victim to the Stalinist purges. Kurella said: "It was hard for me that my own brother was shot. But when I think about it in the larger historical context . . . then maybe it was correct after all." What does he think about it today, now that Khrushchev has exposed the full extent of Stalin's "mistakes" and classified them as crimes?

It is hard for me to have sympathy for people who, when close relatives die a martyr's death, console themselves that the Party must know what is right and just. I remember when KuBa enthusiastically told me one time that comrades were returning from the SU, where they had spent fifteen or more years in prisons or in camps without being guilty of anything. He said their first stop had been the CC: Comrades, here I am again, what should I do? There may be something noble behind such behavior, but I do not understand this mentality. To me they're from a different planet. Brecht said something in *Galileo* like: When an injustice occurs in a city, and no uproar ensues, then it's only fair if the city perishes. When an injustice is done to me or my relatives or friends or a complete stranger, I have to fight back. And if I'm unable to and forbidden to, then I still have to draw conclusions from it. But many people have astonishingly good stomachs—the things they can digest! With what lofty arguments they justify injustice! It's here, in the realm of ethics, that people show their true colors.

2 August 1962   No matter whom one meets at the beach— sentences like this are almost always unavoidable: How can this go on? Can this continue much longer? Where is this taking us? The few loyal, unshakable believers seem like poor lunatics and are viewed and treated as such. You avoid conversations with them. Coupon books for meat have been introduced in Berlin, but the butcher shops are empty. Last weekend, when guests from Berlin arrived here, they said there was neither meat nor sausage, bacon nor butter there. But Ulbricht's agricultural policies are correct, the newspapers write.

People observe a grim silence. They speak out only in trusted circles. The anger vents itself in angry jokes: At a meeting discussion is called for after the speech. No one comes forward.

Finally, after a lot of encouragement, a little old grandmother: "I just wanted to ask," she says, her voice trembling, "is this socialism already or does it get even worse?"

What is a lizard: a crocodile after Party proceedings.

And a herring? A whale after socialism.

And the inquiries to Radio Erivan* coming out of the SU show that the thaw is also proceeding unstoppably there. Everywhere minds are on the move, new forces are stirring; it's only in Albania and the GDR that people are dragging along in the same, old worn-out shoes. And the nauseating part is that our Stalinists deny it and boldly assert that there was no Stalinism in the GDR. How much longer?

Harich's Arrest

After the premiere in Karl-Marx-Stadt on the last weekend in November I spent Sunday with my parents in Bad Schmiedeberg and thus got to the office rather late on Monday. Zöger was not there. He had been urgently called to a meeting with Walter Ulbricht. Janka also showed up late, while Harich had flown to Hamburg the day before, a trip he had had planned for a long time. These were the circumstances: Huffzky, the editor in chief of the West German woman's magazine *Constanze*, was an old acquaintance or even friend of Harich's and had invited him to present his thoughts on the political situation to a circle of interested intellectuals. We had advised Harich to accept the invitation because it gave him the opportunity to acquaint influential and intelligent people with socialist thinking. In court heavy reproaches were leveled against Harich because of this trip and against us for our approval of the undertaking. We had supposedly exposed Party-internal issues to the class-enemy, and so forth. That is, of course, nonsense. The theoretical and practical political problems with which we were occupied in those days were not Party-internal in nature. They were being publicly discussed in Poland, Hungary, and elsewhere. And besides, the people Harich was talking to were not class-enemies but potential allies.

How we ourselves appraised the affair is elucidated by the following incident: a few days before Harich's trip to Hamburg, Zöger and I ate lunch with a comrade responsible for the KPD's work with the intelligentsia there. We informed him of Harich's

---

*A mythical radio station used in jokes; its listeners call in to ask naive political questions.—Tr.

intentions and urged him to make contact with Huffzky and his circle. What Harich really said in Hamburg I do not know. Because he also met with Augstein from *Der Spiegel* and *Der Spiegel* published a well-informed cover story after Harich's arrest, it seems that Harich confided in considerable detail to this journalist.

The whole business with the Hamburg trip did not preoccupy me as much as it did the Stasi later on. We had other worries. Heinz Zöger returned from the CC looking very battered. Ulbricht had summoned the editors in chief of several important newspapers and raked them over the coals. He had attacked *Sonntag* especially ferociously. Zöger had buckled, and committed himself to publishing a self-critical editorial. He then wrote it without consulting me and had it printed as a commentary in the current issue. I protested vehemently, there were violent arguments in the editorial staff, but most people still caved in, since Ulbricht had aimed at us personally. A Party meeting was scheduled for Thursday, 29 November 1956, in which members of the Culture Department of the CC were supposed to participate.

I wanted to resign from the editorial staff, and discussed it with Janka. He was against it: there were so few of us still working and we should not voluntarily retreat. I therefore stayed on and braced myself for a tough fight.

The meeting was set for 2 o'clock in the afternoon. Shortly before it I went once more to Janka to ask him, as director of the publishing house, to take part. Unfortunately he had a prior commitment. With him I found Harich, who had just returned from Hamburg. He was in a splendid mood and in the few minutes remaining reported on his successful visit. He said there was great interest in the West in the attempts to bring Communism out of its Stalinist degeneracy and reform it. He had been invited to write articles in newspapers. We immediately advised against that, since something like that would necessarily discredit our intentions.

When I told Harich about the impending Party meeting he made his usual little jokes: You they'll dismiss and me they'll lock up: that way there will be someone to rehabilitate afterward. A few hours later he had already been arrested and was sitting in the "Hohenschönhausen U-boat," the underground prison of the Stasi . . .

We learned of it at the end of the meeting, which had been very stormy. Zöger had produced a self-critical statement and therefore stood outside the line of fire. All the attacks were aimed at me. I no longer know exactly who was there from the CC. I believe it was Adam, Schlemm, and Lewin. Their marching orders were clear to me: the originator of the false course is Just and the editorial staff must distance themselves from him, while the question of what was to be done with me remained open. But lo and behold: the comrades refused to play along, they closed ranks behind me, declared their collective responsibility. A weak resolution was passed, with which those under instructions declared themselves in disagreement. Further meetings were to follow.

After the meeting I ran into Janka, who told me that Harich had just been arrested. An uncanny feeling crept over me. I saw a connection between that and the day's attack on me. But we were still naive, and thought that Harich had got mixed up in something else. In the official announcement, which appeared in the paper over the next few days, two others were mentioned, Steinberger and Hertwig, whom we did not know. We believed, because we wanted to, that the move against Harich was not directed against us. And as for him, the charges against him seemed so ridiculous to us that we could not believe it would ever come to legal proceedings.

During the next few days the Aufbau-Verlag was like a hornets' nest. Indignation, fear, insecurity, cowardice, valiant defense of an innocent man—every chord was struck. Leading intellectuals like Helene Weigel intervened immediately with Grotewohl. The answer: he said he could not interfere with a case in litigation. Harich remained in custody and we lay low, waiting for the trouble that was sure to come.

18 August 1962

We didn't have long to wait. Walter Janka was arrested exactly one week after Harich. Of course I afterward often asked myself how it happened that we let ourselves be arrested one after the other. Nothing would have been easier than escaping to safety. Later I described to my cellmate the chronological course of events: Harich arrested—I stayed; Janka arrested—I stayed; interrogation by the Stasi—I stayed; Party-proceedings against me— I stayed; dismissal from *Sonntag*—I stayed; summons to appear at Harich's trial—I went to it! Whereupon he said: They should have given you twenty years in prison, not four; so much stupidity has to be punished!—Were we stupid? Naive, yes, because we believed that after the 20th Party Congress it was simply impossible that Stalinist trials like this could still take place. We felt we were right and aligned with the progressive tendencies in the Communist world-movement, and thus overestimated our power and felt safe. We were not conscious of any criminal culpability and deluded ourselves with the illusion that the authorities would have to take the facts of the case into account. As if it had anything to do with facts! Well, we paid dearly for our illusions and naiveté . . .

To characterize the Stasi's illegal methods, the following should be noted: during the week between Harich's and Janka's arrests several Stasi people forced their way into the publishing house one night and compelled the night watchman to hand over the keys to the directors' offices so they could search them. The night watchman (who wasn't even a Party member) was ordered to maintain complete secrecy, under threat of severe repercussions. When Janka discovered traces of the nocturnal raid, the poor watchman suffered such a conflict of conscience that he blurted it all out and immediately afterwards had a nervous breakdown. Janka protested this outrageous incident in a fiery letter to Becher. Becher was likewise indignant and appears to have lodged a complaint somewhere. The result of it was that Janka was promptly arrested, while they took their time with the rest of us.

The Two Minds of Johannes R. Becher

Becher played a shifting role in the Party confrontations of the time and in the struggle for democratization and liberalization. In his heart he of course wished for more liberal and reasonable policies; he was too intelligent not to see what possibilities the Party was forfeiting under Ulbricht's leadership. Thus in 1953 he was one of the spokesmen for a new course in cultural policy, and his early days as Minister of Culture were very promising. On the other hand, he was a personal friend of Ulbricht's. I have never found out what was behind it, but something must have happened while they were emigrés in Moscow that bound Becher inseparably to Ulbricht. One can hardly imagine a more unlikely pair!

Becher essentially agreed with our editorial policies. And I wish I could have seen how he twisted and turned when we were convicted and he received a thrashing because of us! He reacted cautiously to Harich's arrest. Janka's arrest infuriated him. We were having a Party meeting at Aufbau when Günter Caspar called Becher with the news; Caspar subsequently told us that Becher had spoken out very indignantly and wanted to talk to Schirdewan right away. He apparently did so, but without results. And apparently Ulbricht was later able to "convince" him. At Christmas-time Lilly Becher, assuredly not without the knowledge and approval of her husband, sent gifts to Lotte Janka for her children and a potted azalea, with the wish, "May this bloom until this misfortune has passed." I read the letter myself, when I visited Lotte for New Year's. Every line conveyed disapproval of the proceedings against Janka and solidarity with him and his wife.

One day in November, after he had already installed Gysi as a spy among us, Becher invited me to his apartment. I poured my heart out to him about how these infringements of people's rights and deceitful persecution of comrades outraged me. He asked me if I knew the case of Rajk. I had heard about it from Lukács. Becher knew the facts of the case from different sources. Rajk had been induced to make a false confession for the sake of Party discipline and political necessity. He had been promised that for public consumption he would be condemned to death, but would be brought to a safe place where he could live in peace until this difficult period had passed. He believed his executioners and played along. But they murdered him . . . The circumstances of this unprecedented treachery affected Becher very deeply. He fetched a piece of paper from his study and read me a poem about Rajk. It was among his best. I wonder if it will ever be published? At the time I wanted to have it for *Sonntag*, but Becher became angry: That's exactly your problem, you don't always consider when it's appropriate to publish something. It's impermissible and impossible, for example, to publish this poem now, it would be grist to the mills of our adversaries . . . He gave us several casual poems on unimportant themes instead, which we published because they were Becher's.

July 1989 *This poem has not yet been published, and I almost doubt whether it can be found in the Becher Archives in the house where he used to live. The magazine* Sinn und Form *did recently publish a passage that he left out of his* Poetic Confession *at the time. In it he concerns himself with the personal complicity of everyone who knew of Stalin's crimes and kept quiet about them.**

18 August 1962 After my arrest Becher sent a message through his adjutant Thümmler to my wife that she should turn to him if she experienced financial difficulties.

---

*In 1988, *Sinn und Form* published seven pieces by Becher. Entitled "Selbstzensur" (Self-Censorship), the pieces had been composed following the Twentieth Party Congress but were never published during Becher's lifetime. See J.H. Reid, *Writing Without Taboos* (New York: St. Martin's, 1990), p. 152.—Tr.

After our conviction this same Becher then showed a cool and contemptuous attitude towards us in newspaper articles and speeches. Shortly thereafter he became extremely ill and died. A little more courage and firmness would have been helpful, and not just in our case. What in the world drove him to write an obsequious work on Ulbricht during a period when it must have been clear even in the Communist camp that Ulbricht would at best share Stalin's fate? Why could Becher not act as an exponent of a humane, modern direction in German Communism, without worrying about the consequences it might have for him? And what consequences could it have had? He would have avoided the worst fate of all: to fall into disrepute and oblivion as a poet . . .

But I'm talking only about Becher. Did the others act any differently? Janka was their publisher, their old friend. Where were people like Seghers, Bredel, Uhse, and all the others when he fell on hard times? I can report something positive about only one person: Ludwig Renn. He came to see me in the editorial offices shortly after Janka's arrest. He was angry, but controlled himself in his usual reserved way. He asked me how he could send Janka a pack of cigarettes with a greeting. I advised him to try it through the office of the state's attorney. Janka later told me he did receive the greeting. And what that means to a prisoner, someone who feels abandoned by everyone, you can well imagine.

Yes, writers who live in the West did take steps. Günter Weisenborn was with me in the editorial offices at the beginning of December, just after his return from a trip to China. He simply could not understand what they were up to with Janka, and wrote to Grotewohl saying this, without results, of course. In addition, Leonhard Frank, Halldór Laxness, Aragon, Feuchtwanger, and the translator Johannes von Guenther lodged protests.

Our writers deserted us with flying colors. All of them without exception had agreed with our editorial policy for *Sonntag*. Afterwards none of them wanted to know a thing about it.

July 1989   My diary ends here. That is too bad, since all my present-day memories cannot match the immediacy and authenticity of those notes. Many details have disappeared from my memory. Much of it has already taken on a different coloration. Time has marched on. Illusions have turned to dust. Much of my naive, almost gullible attitude of the time is foreign to me now, almost incomprehensible.

On the topic of writers' behavior, I might also add that my wife and I met Anna Seghers in a movie theater in Berlin-Adlershof a few years after my release. We had been neighbors, you could say, and had visited each other frequently during my employment in the CC's Culture Department and the Writers' Union. Her goulash was exquisite, and she loved a bit of juicy gossip. Because she was present as an observer at Harich's trial, at which I was arrested while on the witness stand, my wife had hurried to see her the next day to ask about the exact circumstances. Anna let her in, but self-consciously stammered that she did not know anything and that Gysi lived right across the way . . . Whereupon Heide knew what was what and left the house. And now, years later, we ran into each other in the lobby of the movie theater, greeted one another, and then Anna looked at my wife and said: "Heide, you don't have to look so angry. I spoke up for you so that you could continue to work at the television station . . ." That was probably true, because it was not normal at the time, but rather exceptional that the wife of a man convicted of being an enemy of the state should be allowed to continue to work in television (without, to be sure, her name's being given; as director and editor she went by her maiden name, Heide Draexler).

I shall now, in the summer of 1989, try to reconstruct from memory what could be called our political concept, which the prosecuting authorities of the GDR turned into a counterrevolutionary platform hostile to the state. Furthermore I shall report on the trial and my arrest . . .

III

The Arrest—The Trial—The Years of Captivity

(1989)

My Political Concept

In order to reconstruct my political views of that time, I would need to have the files of the Stasi at my disposal. In month-long interrogations I explicated these views with all the freshness and animation with which they burned in me. Yes, burned, one must say—we felt we were right, had nothing to hide. The realization or at least discussion of our ideas seemed to us fatefully important for the further existence and successful development of socialism. The scorn of the unspeakable Melsheimer during the trial—people like this wanted to save the Party!—could not touch us, because that was precisely what we had in mind. We had Poland's example before our eyes, where the Party had positioned itself at the head of the reform movement and thereby got it underway without bloodshed (Gomulka's later doings are quite another matter). And on the other hand there was Hungary, where the people's anger had vented itself in an uprising because Rákosi had been replaced by Gerö, who was just as bad. To be sure, in our position there was much that was naively enthusiastic, but is it only cold calculation that brings progress? In any case, the interrogators had an easy time with me; I obligingly laid out for them our—or rather my—concept, because I still considered it the only correct conclusion to be drawn from the CPSU's 20th Party Congress. How the interrogator stubbornly endeavored through trick questioning to recast this concept as counterrevolutionary and subversive, I shall depict later.

The galvanizing factor was, as mentioned, the 20th Party Congress. The official party line on Stalin's crimes and the distortion of socialism fell on fertile ground with us. For us, as for many, socialism was the longed-for culmination of humanism, of the little man, of the centuries-long striving of the noblest minds to bring about the well-being of mankind; it represented the fulfillment of the great utopian concept that only a genuinely humane society without oppression and exploitation in any form could keep the world, with its growing population, from perishing. That is constantly emphasized in the theoretical writings, and Stalin's own works are full of these maxims—but in practice!

Ulbricht made it easy for himself. The sum total of his reaction to the 20th Party Congress consisted in two memorable aphorisms: "We did not have a cult of personality in the GDR," and "From this moment on, Stalin is no longer a classic." And everything was able to and expected to continue as before. What thinking person could that satisfy? Was it not time to analyze the whole system of

Stalinism, to determine the causes for the distortion of socialist ideas? It simply could not have been the doing of a single tyrant. He had millions of helpers, many of them certainly with the best intentions. The notion of a "period of the cult of personality" seemed euphemistic and trivializing to us. Stalinism is a whole system of ideas, behavioral patterns, and actions that is profoundly alien to the essence of socialism.

Klaus Gysi, Becher's appointed watchdog for us, wrote in the New Year's issue of *Sonntag* 1957: "To speak of Stalinism is harmful, splits the workers' movement, and moreover disrupts the cooperation of the forces for peace, because this concept is utterly false; it muddles perceptions. Why? Criticism of the cult of personality around Stalin and of Stalin himself was and is a criticism of certain errors that contradict the socialist order, are alien and harmful to it, without ever having compromised that order as a whole."

That was, and still is today, the argument of the Stalinists, because they themselves thereby remain above criticism, which applied only to Stalin and ended there.

Our thoughts, however, revolved around the question of what the causes and concrete manifestations of Stalinism are, including and above all in the GDR, and what peaceful reforms are necessary to free socialism from them. Passionate discussions, such as were undoubtedly being conducted everywhere in socialist intellectual circles in all countries. The party leadership of the SED did everything to suppress such discussions, so that they would not spread to wider Party circles. How the mass of Party members came to terms with the revelations about Stalin is still a mystery to me. The ignorance and lack of interest among the Party rank and file made it easy for the Stalinists in the SED to settle up with the "recalcitrants," to isolate and silence them.

In addition to these deliberations on Stalinism, which were also engaged in by the reformers in our brother countries (in Poland, for example, more radically), for us there was the further question of national identity. We clung to German unity while avoiding the concept of "reunification," because it denoted the re-establishment of something for which German democrats and socialists could not wish. We saw an opportunity for a socialist GDR, as we wished and imagined it, to become the driving force behind a unified, democratic, neutral, and ultimately unarmed Germany. Or, as Georg Lukács formulated it at the Writers' Congress, the "German Piedmont." As I reflect after more than thirty years on our thinking of the time, I recognize that it has not lost any of its appropriateness. If the left in both German states does not address the national concern of the Germans, namely, the desire to live in a common state, then the right wing will do so, and is well (or disastrously) on its way to doing just that. In practical terms we saw the possibility of a German confederation of provinces east and west. We were convinced that in the five provinces of the GDR we would succeed in keeping a stable majority even in free elections. With the proviso, of course, that in all provinces measures would be taken that one could characterize as "democratization."

Democratization
(excerpt)

The primary aim of democratization consists in promoting the creative participation of all segments of the population in building socialism, that is, to make the issue of socialism an issue for every individual citizen, to an even greater degree than previously. We must succeed in creating a true relationship of trust between the citizens and the administrative organs of the state; to achieve this, we must overcome in the former the spirit of servility, the flight into private life and passivity, and eradicate in the latter all arrogance, schoolmasterly preaching, and administrative paternalism. Democratization from below must meaningfully complement democratization from above. The socialist democracy requires that the society's functionaries, by virtue of their qualifications and larger overview, fulfill their leadership assignments unpretentiously and in the spirit of the people, attentively study and take to heart the experiences of the masses in building socialism, consult with those affected on all of their measures and explain these measures to them. It would also be appropriate if we availed ourselves of modern technology even more than hitherto. It would make a great impression if the members of our government and other leading figures informed the population over radio and television in simple, jargon-free statements, person to person so to speak, about their thinking, their plans and the challenges in their area of competence, not only in conjunction with important events, but regularly. We must see to that as many citizens of our state as possible take democratization into their own hands, utilizing more energetically than heretofore our abundant possibilities. Every citizen can come into his own. In the organizations of the Cultural League and in the clubs of the intelligentsia, for example, intellectuals have the opportunity to articulate issues that trouble them, and with the help of the Cultural League, specifically its representatives, eliminate deficiencies and implement improvements.

There can be no discussion about whether or not we are progressing in building socialism. In the course of socialist democratization we are interested only in the question of how, consistent with conditions and traditions in Germany, we can best strengthen socialism within the various aspects of life. It is only natural that in this matter, even among the socialists and the progressives allied with them, there should be differences of opinion; working through them in an unbiased, sober manner will promote precisely this process of democratization and the participation of independent minded and responsible citizens.

—G.J.

—*Sonntag*, 11 November 1956

As we saw it, the most important factor in the building of socialism in the GDR (the necessity of which we never doubted) was to carry out societal, political, and economic reorganization in such a way that it could be understood, assented to, and supported by workers in all of Germany. And not only by the workers, but also by the leftists—social democrats and left-wing liberals. The prevailing anti-fascism in the GDR offered a solid foundation for winning over precisely these groups. By including social democrats we were admittedly stirring up a hornets' nest. That always made the Stalinists see red and probably always will. (When the Soviet magazine *Sputnik* dared in November 1988 to point out that the KPD's struggle in the '20s and '30s—under Stalin's orders—against the SPD, the "socialist fascists," had abetted Hitler's seizure of power, the SED had the audacity to ban this widely-read magazine in spite of the resulting protest. Later they came up with a counterargument: the Comintern had already corrected its misdirected policy by 1935—true, but by then the Nazis had been in power for three years!).

When during the spring of 1946 the SPD, partly voluntarily and partly under duress, merged with the KPD, the resulting new party, the SED, promised to become a genuine synthesis of both parties, keeping the virtues of both and avoiding the mistakes of both. At least that was the version I heard when I joined the SED in July 1946. The Westerhausen town committee consisted mainly of former Social Democrats who believed this explanation and were willing to work in good faith with the former Communists. I was even more amazed, as a young comrade, that a considerable number of Social Democrats, probably around twenty, did not join, among them the most respected, people who had known Bebel personally. In many conversations I endeavored to win them over to the SED, but without success. They listened to me, liked and valued me, but they did not waver from their conviction that sooner or later the SED would become a purely communist party, which was not the place for them. They did not stint with warnings about my "noble communism," as they termed it. All of them then joined the local chapter of the Cultural League that I founded, naturally not for the sake of culture, as I thought, but in order to have their meetings be legal. Later that was held very much against me.

Then came the campaign for a new type of party, the bolshevization of the SED, and the chief enemy turned out to be social democracy. The battle was waged not only with words and arguments: thousands of Social Democrats were disciplined, exiled to the West, or thrown into prison. Soviet agencies took an active part in this. Material on all of this certainly exists; it is, however, unavailable to me. I hope that honest historians will one day shed light on this dark chapter in the history of the workers' movement, for which the Stalinists bear complete responsibility.

We thus came to feel that everything here that was criticized by the Social Democrats was worthy of reflection and reexamination. The Stalinists couldn't have cared less how their policies went over in their own country, as well as abroad. And when the Communists' support in the Federal Republic shrank from 10%, which they attained in elections in several districts in the first years after the war, to 0.1%, even that did not jolt them into reflection, into self-awareness. Thus we came to reject everything created and maintained only under duress, by violent means. Why use force to drive the farmers into collectives? Wasn't there a chance that the farmers would embrace the idea of collectives on the strength of their own experience? One had to accustom them to it gradually. The German traditions of farmers' credit unions, dairy and other cooperatives offered possibilities. Shared ownership of heavy machinery, such as harvest combines, etc., buyers' and suppliers' cooperatives, all those things existed and were there to be developed. The leadership must have known what catastrophic consequences forced collectivization had had in the thirties for the standard of living in the Soviet Union. The model should have worked: in every district one or two LPGs managed by competent cadres, supplied with the machinery of the MTS, which the LPGs would not only use for their own purposes, but would also rent out to individual farmers, thereby making them dependent on them. The idea was to get the machinery closer to the actual producers, so that one could dissolve the MTS (which actually occurred later on).

For industry we espoused the Yugoslav model, insofar as we were acquainted with it: self-management and in-house leadership of firms, and works councils selected by all employees, which in turn would choose the plant managers. Centralized state planning should limit itself to key areas of production, above all to heavy industry: mining, energy, metallurgy, and the like. Also to those areas of production that by nature cannot return profits. Because we were not knowledgeable about political economy, we called upon Harich (he had offered to put our ideas in writing) to consult an expert. That Harich chose poor Steinberger for it, who had just returned from a Soviet prison camp and thus became implicated in the so-called Harich Affair and so, like all of us, was sentenced to a long period of imprisonment, I learned only during interrogation while awaiting trial.

That the Yugoslav model, as has become apparent, also did not work, is of no importance. First of all, it was applied in an industrially backward country and second, it was not pursued consistently. In any case it gives me satisfaction that the initiatives in the present policy of *perestroika* are moving in the same direction we had in mind. In this context one should call upon the theories of Ota Sik from the year 1968. I do not know them well enough to permit myself a judgment, but the concept of "socialist market economy" appeals to me.

It also fills me with satisfaction that in the Soviet Union they now view the forced collectivization of the '30s in a thoroughly critical fashion and are trying through lease arrangements to implement a limited reprivatization, while keeping collective ownership of land. Now our state and party leaders say: Collectivization in the GDR stood the test, the LPGs flourished. That may be, and today nobody has any thoughts of rescinding anything. But was all the coercion, the forced pace necessary? Did we have to make thousands of farmers' families unhappy, drive many of them out of the country? And what about the cooperative consciousness of LPG members? Do not all too many of them feel like farmhands, admittedly better paid than under the old landholders, but equally alienated from the land and livestock? Does the LPG farmer feel like the head of the farm, does the worker feel like the owner of the state-owned factory? That, after all, is the measure of the superiority of socialism over capitalism.

When Brecht recommended experimenting with different models, we, Zöger and I, had the previously mentioned conversation at Brecht's house on the best way to regulate the mechanics of productive operations. That we did not find the philosophers' stone can be seen in present-day developments in the Soviet Union and in other countries, where people are experimenting and searching for optimal solutions. To the Stalinists, however, this sort of experimentation is an unacceptable demand. They know everything and are always right. Any uncertainty is a sign of unforgivable weakness. Not a single key issue concerning societal developments in the GDR was ever genuinely discussed with the people. Not once was an alternative presented: universal conscription or a professional army, private or collectivized agriculture, German unity or sealing the border, comprehensive school or a diversified school system—the list goes on. Thus the press was always compelled to play the role of mouthpiece for the Party and state leadership. We believed, however, that the press should publish opposing views, including critical ones, as a mouthpiece of the groups in society for which this or that newspaper was intended. We accordingly saw it as our job as the editors of *Sonntag* not only to explain to the intellectuals the cultural policy formulated by the Party leadership and to win them over, but also to provide space for their critical objections, to take up unresolved challenges, to put questions to the leadership. We were sharply rebuked for this, having allegedly offered a platform to vacillating intellectuals.

Similarly, problematic issues arose in connection with the mass organizations. Here Lenin's concept of a "transmission belt" prevailed. That meant in practice that the only motor, the only driving force, is the Party (and within it the top leadership), which, with the help of this belt, transfers movement to the masses, which would otherwise be lifeless and inactive. The consequence is to ignore every movement within the "masses," to discredit it as a manifestation of "spontaneity" and thus to suppress it. The only result can be a lack of interest among the population, extending to lethargy, as we witness it today in all the fully socialist countries. People feel disenfranchised because they "in any case have nothing to say." With remarkable perspicacity Rosa Luxemburg foresaw this unfortunate development and described it in her article "Dictatorship and Democracy," but nowhere did the Stalinists take seriously the handwriting on the wall. We thus felt that the Trade Union Federation should advocate more vigorously for the vital interests of the workers, and that applied equally to the DFD, the Cultural League, and the FDJ, with respect to the groups they represented.

The FDJ played a special role in our thinking, especially for me as a former member of the *Bündische Jugend*. We recognized that this organization neither represented the broad interests of youth, nor understood how to organize a way of life suitable for young people and bring all the youth together on a voluntary basis. Many joined the FDJ only to get ahead professionally, to secure themselves a place at the university, even to get into extended secondary school, which would make them eligible for the *Abitur*. How were Christian youth supposed to find a niche in an organization that viewed itself single-mindedly as the SED's training auxiliary? Meanwhile they called their governing body a parliament, which already expresses a sort of pluralism. I held that the FDJ should be an umbrella organization for various groups: Red Boy Scouts, Christian Boy Scouts, socialist students, liberal students, et al., which would have acknowledged the fact that other parties were operating besides the SED, even if they were tied to the SED's apron strings. That could change—according to the jointly adopted constitution, each is allowed to develop its own personality. Today I am convinced that sooner or later such an evolution will be unavoidable in the GDR.

More democracy, less bureaucracy. More emphasis on the self-determining citizen, less on the state. And democracy without pluralism is impossible. Pluralism of beliefs does not suffice. An individual can believe all he wants, but the question remains: Where and how can he express his beliefs? In a closed room, in a circle of friends? In that case, he has no influence. For that there must also be organizational pluralism. Either several parties that unite and represent people with shared opinions, or, if the one-party system is retained, fractions within the Party. In reality they were always there; they were simply not allowed to marshal themselves. It would be abnormal if a communist movement (of all things!) did not have a conservative and a reform wing. The bloody suppression of all non-Stalinists by Stalin was intended as a permanent warning in the form of a terrifying example. We stayed on the side of the reform wing vis-à-vis the prevailing scheme; we were the "leftists."

Less emphasis on the state, that meant among other things getting rid of censorship. Over the years, as publishing developed in the GDR, qualified editors and editors in chief had achieved so much expertise that one could trust them to decide which books should be published. This decision can and may be guided only by the paragraphs in the constitution that forbid, among other things, race-baiting, warmongering, and incitement to assassination.

Less emphasis on the state, that means dismantling the huge and exponentially increasing bureaucracy, the *Apparat*. Many staffers seemed superfluous or at least too well supplied with subordinates. (Here I am reminded of a conversation I recently had with the former foreign minister of Czechoslovakia, Bohuslav Chnoupek, a book of whose I translated. A drastic reduction of the central bureaucracy had just been decided upon in the Soviet Union. Shevardnadze, the Soviet foreign minister, had told him that he was being forced to discharge approximately half his staff; he said he could do that quite easily, since they did nothing anyway.)

Reorganizing the political economy according to our concept would have rendered superfluous a number of ministries concerned with industry. Culture and popular education were to be combined in one ministry and reduced considerably in size. The universities and technical schools were to be steered by a "council" made up of the presidents of these educational establishments, with a small executive secretariat. Self-administration, a system of local councils in all areas. A particular thorn in our side was the Ministry for State Security, which we held primarily responsible for the many breaches of legality. If we had known that we would soon come into personal contact with this sinister apparatus, this state within a state, perhaps we would have been more cautious. (I do not think so, however; there was no going back: Here I stand, I cannot do otherwise . . .) Neither in the Imperial Reich nor in the Weimar Republic had there been such an institution. It runs counter to German traditions, leaving aside the Nazis' *Reichssicherheitshauptamt* and the Gestapo. We did not, of course, want essential aspects of state security to be neglected. But agencies already existed to take care of them: espionage and counter-espionage belonged to the military, the struggle against political crimes (sabotage, boycotts, and other forms of harassment) could be pursued in a special investigative department of the criminal police (in the Weimar Republic it was called m. E. K5). And everything else, spying on the people and other things the Stasi does, was to be abolished as unconstitutional.

Once they had us in their clutches, the Stasi exacted retribution from us twice over for these ideas: on the one hand, despite all the facts and the defense's motion for acquittal, they procured our conviction and the most severe terms of imprisonment (years of solitary confinement), while on the other hand they wanted to demonstrate to us how properly they behaved: house searches with witnesses chosen by my wife, interrogations only during the day, never under duress—they had plenty of time—which was unnecessary anyway, since we confessed to our views with the clearest of consciences.

There remains the question of the people involved. I would have no need to go into it, if a passage in Erich Loest's book *Durch die Erde ein Riss* (The Earth Cracks) had not given rise to misunderstandings. In contrast to me, Loest was not in solitary confinement and was badgered by his fellow prisoners to explain what was really going on with him and the Harich Group. No one wanted to believe that we were merely developing theories and did not aspire to power. To get rid of his troublesome questioners, Loest threw them a juicy tidbit: "Out of malice or as a joke he (Loest) often began his account with the ridiculous assertion, with which Mach, the public prosecutor, had begun the indictment: I wanted to overthrow the government.—At that it grew quiet; they pricked up their ears and asked which position L. had picked out for himself, for why would one overthrow a government if one did not want a place at the trough? Whereupon L. had made up an answer: Harich wanted to become first secretary of the SED and Janka prime minister, Just foreign minister . . . " (Loest, *Durch die Erde ein Riss*, page 403).

Of course not a word of that is true. As far as cadres were concerned, our discussion focused only on the question: Who could be a "German Gomulka," putting these ideas (being discussed at the time among almost all Party intellectuals) into practice as Party policy? That such a thing would never come about under Ulbricht's leadership was abundantly clear to us. He was certainly acceptable as a member of a new, collective Party leadership, but not as leader. Lenin's warning about Stalin applied to him, mutatis mutandis. We knew too little about the other members of the Party leadership, but we could not imagine that all of them fully agreed with Ulbricht's aloof response to the 20th Party Congress. In our judgment, the leader would have to be a primus inter pares and be presented as someone who had been unjustly persecuted like Gomulka and therefore had a certain credibility with the people. Paul Merker and Franz Dahlem came to mind. My conversation with Merker on the Day of Repentance in 1956 made it clear that he was not prepared to return to political life. It caused me never-ending regret that through this meeting we got him involved in our trial, where he had to appear as a witness, being shouted at and threatened by Melsheimer, who said he might well find himself appearing as a defendant again.

Thus the question of who in the SED leadership could guide a course suggested by the direction of the CPSU's 20th Party Congress left us at a loss. But it was also not our job to worry about it. All the charges suggesting that we wanted to overthrow Ulbricht are pure nonsense. We were not politicians but theoreticians. I repeatedly insisted that we give up our fruitless, circular, often highly emotional discussions and put our thoughts in writing and send them to the CC as a basis for discussion. Harich declared himself ready to do the writing part. Later I made the suggestion, based on my experience working in the Party apparatus, that we send the write-up to the monthly magazine *Einheit*. The editorial staff would not publish what we submitted, but would pass it on the CC, which was what we intended.

I never saw Harich's detailed exposition with my own eyes. His arrest intervened. So I do not know whether his version coincided in every detail with my ideas. Because we never discussed our ideas as a total concept, I also cannot say to what extent Janka and Zöger were in agreement with me. On basic questions, on the general thrust we were certainly united: more democracy, more humane procedures, more effectiveness in the sciences, policies aimed at a unified, democratic Germany open to socialist development.

The main points of our concept may be summed up as follows:

—reestablishing the provinces, as a stage preliminary to confederation;

—reducing economic planning to the setting of targets, production of raw materials, and direction of key industries (mining, metallurgy, transportation, energy);

—independence of production facilities, efficient accounting processes, workers' councils, elected plant managers, market relationships among the production facilities;

—no forced collectivization of agriculture; instead encouragement of traditional German cooperative models, dissolving the MTSs and transferring their equipment to the agricultural cooperatives;

—dissolving several ministries concerned with industry;

—reducing administrative bureaucracy;

—leadership of universities and technical schools by a "council of presidents," with the goal of reestablishing the traditional autonomy of these educational institutions;

—abolishing censorship;

—shifting the duties of the Ministry for State Security to the Interior and Defense Ministries;

—ending the use of coercive measures against the churches;

—converting the FDJ into an umbrella organization for various youth groups;

—stronger representation of the interests of members by the mass organizations;

—authorizing more associations through a law on associations;

—truthful, public coverage by the press of all problems affecting people.

The list is incomplete, certainly contestable in some particulars because they are unrealistic. But imagine such ideas being discussed publicly, so that specialists from every field could speak out! We allowed ourselves to be guided only by old-fashioned common sense and the precepts of Marxism-Leninism, which we had mastered through study and, like Janka, in hard class struggle. Janka in particular could draw upon decades of experience. Also Zöger. I had graduated from Party schools and had worked in the Party apparatus. Harich was a highly-educated theoretician, philosopher, and aesthetician. Without any great effort we could have supported our ideas with the teachings of Lenin, if only there had been a real discussion.

Like us in our circle, hundreds if not thousands of people at the time—in the GDR, in the other people's democracies, and in the Soviet Union, in the whole communist movement—were debating how one could free socialism from its Stalinist deformations. What a display of creative energy, which could have become a perceptible force, was nipped in the bud by those unteachable, incorrigible Stalinists! In the GDR alone, how many comrades and sympathizers were expelled from editorial staffs and professorships, thrown out of the Party, put in prison, or driven to the West. Had the thaw of 1956 been able to spread to all socialist countries, had it not been frozen in a forcibly imposed ice age, how differently the Soviet Union and its allies would be positioned today! Gorbachev would be having an easier time with his *perestroika*, if indeed it had not long since become reality. But in history "What if . . . " does not count. History staggers along, often going astray and getting on the wrong track, but eventually finding its way to that to which mankind consciously or unconsciously aspires. Of this optimistic view of history no bitter experience can rob me . . .

As a Witness in Harich's Trial

I spent the last days of February and the first days of March 1957 with my parents in Bad Schmiedeberg. By mutual agreement with the secretariat of the Cultural League, I had resigned from *Sonntag*. They graciously continued to pay my salary until the end of March. I began to work on several literary projects that I had been wanting to get to for a long time. In Bad Schmiedeberg I wrote the foregoing diary. In Berlin I had not dared to work on it because I could never be sure that stout knaves from the Stasi would not suddenly ring the bell and undertake a house search. After all, when still in my job as editor, I had once been summoned to an almost day-long "conversation," from which I had had to conclude that they already had me in their sights as well. Harich arrested, Janka arrested; why was I still free? In all seriousness, I confess that I did not believe that I was in danger. On the contrary, I was convinced that both of them would be released at any moment. An error, an usurpation of power by ultrareactionaries who had not understood which way the wind was blowing. What naiveté!

Thus, when I was subpoenaed as a witness, I was determined to testify truthfully in the trial against Harich, because that would have to convince the court that dismissing the case was the only proper course of action. On 7 March, at the beginning of the actual trial, we witnesses were simply called forward and admonished to testify truthfully. Then we were sent home.

The following day, 8 March, the International Day of Women, we had to reappear. My wife fixed a delicious roast duck for dinner because I would not be away long. With a clear conscience yet a pounding heart I entered the courthouse. On the steps Anna Seghers and Helene Weigel caught up with me. Along with other intellectuals, they were attending the proceedings as observers. They pressed my hand encouragingly, but could not conceal how worried they were. Evidently, from the way the trial had gone up to then, they sensed that something unpleasant was in store for me. In the witness room, several of us huddled together dejectedly, among us Heinz Zöger, who after my departure from the editorial staff had obediently carried on, following the Party line; Erich Wendt, who had taken over direction of the Aufbau-Verlag after Janka's arrest; and others whom I have forgotten. No one spoke to anyone else; a tense atmosphere prevailed. The fact that we were not permitted to leave the room without permission contributed to this atmosphere, for it was as if we were already under arrest. Erich Wendt looked especially downcast; I later learned that Stalinist justice had also had him in its clutches. He knew what was in store for him.

It was like a deliverance from the agonizing suspense when I was finally—it was almost evening—called to the witness stand. Some witness stand—in an open space one had to step up to—or rather, under—the bench, the microphone in front, and high above one, the judges in their black robes. I plucked up all my courage, for I wanted to help Harich prove his innocence. I was asked about several details of our concept and answered willingly. Mention was constantly made of a "platform," a "group," and I knew only all too well from my study of the CPSU's history where such formulations were leading; I strenuously resisted them, as also later at the interrogation. I was taken by surprise when they asked whether I had known that Harich intended to publicize our platform by way of RIAS. I did not know exactly what was meant until it occurred to me: "That wasn't it. When I asked Harich to put our ideas in writing and send the statement as an article to *Einheit* or the CC, he said: 'But we have to threaten the CC that if they do not discuss the article, we will send it to RIAS.'"

"Aha!" screamed the chief prosecutor. "So you knew what Harich intended!"

I replied that that had not been Harich's intention, but an empty threat that I had not taken seriously. The CC would have had us arrested immediately if we had included such an idiotic threat in our letter. I had said so to Harich, and the point had never been raised again.

Thereupon Melsheimer stood up, from head to toe the embodiment of state power, and bawled out—for criminals like us he had no other tone: "If you had attended the proceedings up to now, you would understand why I am now having you arrested!"

Although I should have been expecting something like this, his words hit me like a blow to the head. I went through the next hours, the next days half-stunned, as in a nightmare. I remember only that I gasped: "This can't be true!" Then I had to approach the judges' bench, had to deposit my papers, wallet, wristwatch, and wedding ring—for what reason I still do not know; I have never seen anything similar in a movie or in a book. I remember the ring so clearly because for quite some time I had not been able to slip it off—I had gained weight and the ring was stuck on my finger. And now it slid off just like that—the cold sweat that had broken out over my entire body served as a lubricant.

Then I was led away and pushed into a pigeonhole with bars. Everything had been prepared well in advance. And who should appear in the cell next to mine but good old Zöger. It must have hit him even harder; he had shown good will and proper humility, and now he was reaping such ingratitude for his cooperative attitude. Melsheimer had turned the show trial into an impressive demonstration—two witnesses arrested in the courtroom: that proved how dangerous these traitors to socialism were! And it undoubtedly served its purpose—to intimidate the audience (insofar as they were not there under orders from the Party and the Stasi) and to crush any thoughts of political alternatives. And of course for both of us it meant that a guilty verdict was inevitable.

I did not sleep a wink that night. My thoughts circled endlessly, fluttering like birds in a cage, which was where I now in fact found myself. The so-called holding cell, to which I was then moved, was a cramped, windowless hole where one could not help being terrified. It came as a relief when I was transferred the next morning to the Stasi's pre-trial detention facility in Hohenschönhausen. Where this chamber of horrors is located and what it looks like from the outside, I do not know to this day. Later I learned from my sometime cellmate Benno Szuminski that the prisoners called it the U-boat. The cells are underground. The tiny barred windows near the ceiling are at ground level.

Pre-Trial Detention

First I was left to stew for a few days. Then I was brought before a man who introduced himself as the prison magistrate. Oddly enough, he performed his duties in the Stasi's prison itself, so what kind of a magistrate could he have been! A Stasi officer played this role so that everything would seem to take a legal course; that was, after all, a major point in our conception of the re-establishment of legal procedure and the abolition of the special privileges that the Stasi, without the knowledge of the public, had arrogated to itself. This "magistrate" revealed to me that I would be kept in custody because of the risk of escape and suppression of evidence. I objected, saying that I was innocent and had not the slightest reason to suppress anything, because there was nothing to suppress. And if I had wanted to flee the country, I could have done it long since if I had had a guilty conscience, at the latest when Harich and Janka were arrested. My objection was noted without comment. Nothing was changed in my case; its course had been fixed long ago.

I was kept in pre-trial detention for almost half a year. It took the gentlemen of the Stasi, in cooperation with the prosecutor general's office, that long to cobble together the charges. I was summoned for interrogation almost every day. The transcript must contain thousands of pages. For the most part I had the same interrogator, a basically pleasant fellow whose name and rank I of course never learned. At first I saw in him a comrade whom I would surely soon convince that we were concerned not with ambitions hostile to the Party or even the state, but rather exclusively with ideas; ideas that came from comrades devoted to the Party because they believed that the Party urgently needed reform, and that they had to position themselves in the vanguard of the people's desire for reform—as had been done in Poland, so that what had happened in Hungary would not happen here as well.

My naiveté soon dissipated, however, as I realized more and more clearly that this interrogator was playing a deceitful game with me. He used the most ordinary tricks to dupe me. For example, he chatted with me cordially about how I pictured a reform of agricultural policy. I readily explained my views to him. Then he picked up a pen and paper: "All right, now let's get this all down." I obligingly dictated to him what I had to say, which he now and then corrected or expanded; sometimes I accepted his changes, sometimes not. Then he presented me with the hand-written pages for my signature. To my astonishment I read the following heading, formulated by him: "In what ways did the subversive, counterrevolutionary group want to obstruct the collectivization of agriculture?" I, of course, said I would not sign it because the very way the question was phrased was malicious slander. Whereupon he said I was not responsible for the question, merely for the answer. Whereupon I asked if he refused to recognize that answering such a question represented an acknowledgment that we were a group, and a counterrevolutionary, subversive one at that. Besides, we of course did not want to obstruct collectivization, but rather see it carried out in a way that would be consistent with German tradition. He became indignant, furious, because he knew that his boss would be angry with him. But I stood my ground; the question had to be reformulated. And so it went, without respite, in an exhausting back and forth; often we would engage in a day-long tug-of-war over one sentence. I thought everything depended on it; I still could not believe that they would charge us on the basis of such shabby, far-fetched misinterpretations. And I did not know that, one way or another, my fate had already been sealed.

To go through these interrogations, not to give in, not to capitulate, took a tremendous amount of effort. My original attitude, that I was dealing with a comrade to whom I had only to clarify my ideas in order to convince him of my legal innocence, soon yielded to this insight: There sits my enemy, who wants to get me by the throat, who will use every means from friendly persuasion to the most banal tricks and threats. The fight was uneven. He had an entire apparatus behind him, he represented the ruling power, went home at night to his family, perhaps going out with them to the movies, the theater, or a concert, arriving in the morning freshly shaven and rested "for work." I was led back to my cell, isolated, cut off from the outside world, tormented by worry about my wife and two children—Martin (who was ten at the time) and Katharina (who was seven), who must be missing their father—poorly fed; the suit I had been arrested in soon hung on me. In my cell, which measured approximately fifty-five square feet, the electricity had to be on all the time because scarcely any light came in through the tiny window up near the ceiling, which was always filthy on the outside. The back wall was taken up by the cot, on which one was allowed only to sit during the day. In the unoccupied space in front, measuring approximately eighteen square feet, one could walk back and forth and do calisthenics. For relieving oneself there was a bucket in the corner, a degrading set-up. One could lie down only after the bellowed command "Bedtime!" which I estimate was given around 9 o'clock. Often one was abruptly wakened at night because one had inadvertently put one's arms and hands under the blankets, which was forbidden. In the morning they roused us with the shout "On your feet!" How the logistics of washing and receiving meals were handled, I have forgotten completely. For my hour of recreation, which lasted fifteen to twenty minutes, I was taken alone to a small courtyard enclosed by high walls. In the entire time of my pre-trial detention I never saw another prisoner face to face, apart from the confrontations in court with Harich and Zöger. The only people I had to talk with were the interrogator, then several times his boss, an even more despicable type, then several times Prosecutor General Jahnke, an ice-cold bureaucrat, and shortly before the main trial Melsheimer.

So: an uneven fight. And a hopeless and ultimately senseless one. If I had refused to make any statement, the result would not have changed. But who can survive something like that? Ulbricht needed to make an example, and he had us. The verdict had been decided long ago. The so-called investigation was a joke, as was the trial itself. How much effort, how much work expended to keep up the sham: my appearances before the "prison magistrate," the recording of transcripts, every page of which I had to sign individually, and then again in the clean copy, "so that nothing can be falsely attributed to me," as the interrogator ingratiatingly informed me. Every transcript marked with the starting and ending time of the interrogation, only days, never nights, exactly as prescribed, confrontation with the other defendants. Altogether a flawless production whose directors surely deserved applause. What role did we play in it? Certainly not that of real actors, for otherwise we would not have entered pleas of "not guilty" at the trial and persuaded our defense attorneys to move for acquittal.

It was also part of this farce that, as a prisoner awaiting trial, I was granted rights of which others (according to my later cellmate Benno) could not have dreamed: Heide was allowed to send me edibles, within limits—mostly nourishing pralines. Pralines in the

U-boat, can you picture that! Every week a guard would appear with a hamper full of books, and I was allowed to pick one out. My wife was also permitted to send me a book; it was "Orders from On High" by Ehm Welk. In my naiveté I believed that it had come from Ehm Welk himself, with whom I had cultivated friendly relations in my erstwhile functions. My impression was erroneous, just like the hope that so many intellectuals with whom I had had dealings would stand up in some way for me, for us. Far from it! They had been shown the instruments of torture, and that sufficed.

In mid-May I had a discussion with Dr. Pein, a lawyer from Arnstadt whom Heide, on the advice of Janka's defense lawyer, Friedrich Wolff, had retained for me. To this end I was brought to the Stasi prison in Lichtenberg, which I would get to know much better later on. Unfortunately, Dr. Pein, who made a very good impression on Heide and me and was fully convinced of my legal innocence, had to give up the case a few days before the trial because he had been assigned to a major case in Erfurt involving economic issues. To what extent this was done intentionally, I am unable to say.

It may sound strange, but as nerve-wracking as the interrogations were, the days when I was not summoned seemed to me the greater torture. In the interrogations one could do something, one could fight, even when, in the final analysis, it was pointless. Worse was condemnation to utter inactivity, because one's thoughts circled around one thing only: How can I prove to them that our aspirations were directed at strengthening socialism and not weakening or even undermining it?

The Easter holidays of 1957 are dreadful memories to me. I can well imagine that a person might buckle under the strain, and have a mental breakdown. Now and then I almost lost touch with reality. At such times it seemed to me that I needed only to go to the door, and it would open by itself. One incident remains unforgotten. It was on 7 July, and a powerful storm with gale winds was raging as evening approached. Around 7 o'clock—somehow one could feel the time—the storm blew down the high wall I could see through the almost opaque window. The wall collapsed on 7/7 at 7 o'clock! And me in cell number 7! If that was not a good omen! The hope that I would be released soon turned into a euphoric certainty. The disenchantment was all the more depressing when everything continued as before. And they had so much time. No one was breathing down their necks. Yes, they had time. A statement I heard often, much too often, whenever I turned somewhat obstinate and insisted on my formulation.

Melsheimer took the final interrogation himself. I have seldom sat across from such a repugnant human being. Bloated, crude, cynical. He kept gulping down some kind of pills. He had only two topics of conversation: Harich's threat to broadcast over RIAS if the CC would not discuss our concept; in Melsheimer's construction it was Harich's firm intention. A misguided distortion, but it sufficed for setting a legal trap for us. The second topic was Harich's visits to the SPD in West Berlin and to the SPD's Eastern bureau. I did not know anything about these visits. Whereupon Melsheimer challenged: "We know that, that you didn't know anything about them. But in a gang of thieves, even the gang doesn't always know what the leader is doing."

After this interrogation, I knew for certain that my trial was imminent. I received the list of charges, which I was allowed to keep for one day—an indescribable concoction that will be discussed later on.

As a humorous sidelight, one more precautionary measure taken by our jailers: a week before the main trial I was taken to the infirmary every day and exposed for longer and longer periods to a sunlamp. As I was able to conclude from Janka's, Zöger's, and Wolf's lightly-tanned complexions, this cosmetic benefit was also provided for them. As one can see, the Stasi does everything for you.

The Trial Against Janka, Just, Zöger, and Wolf

When the indictment was handed down, I was promoted from being accused to being formally indicted. That was tangibly expressed when handcuffs were clapped on me immediately after I left the cell. Everything by the book. I was unexpectedly given an opportunity to speak to my new defense attorney, Frau Dr. Schindowski. Since she had already dealt with Zöger's file, she understood the situation somewhat. But now she was facing an almost insoluble problem: Zöger wanted to show remorse, to acknowledge contritely his sins against Party and state in order to come away with a lesser sentence (which he succeeded in doing), but I wanted to fight, to point out the injustice of it, to prove my innocence and be acquitted. Without our having conferred on the matter, that was also Janka's intention. Now Frau Schindowski had to defend two clients charged with the same offense, each of whom wanted to pursue his defense differently. She urged me to accept Zöger's approach, but in vain. Subsequently, she must have persuaded Zöger to adopt our posture, which he then did willingly.

Clean-shaven, tanned, and in handcuffs, I was driven to the High
Court on 23 July. They put me into a spacious cell with Zöger,
whom I was now seeing again for the first time since our
confrontation in court in the spring. He appeared depressed, but told
me that, contrary to his original intention, he would likewise plead
not guilty.

Before the trial began, they brought me into another room where
my interrogator was waiting for me. He asked me in a very friendly
way if I had any questions, whether we should not go over this or
that one more time. Apparently it was also very important for him
that I play my role as the Stasi wanted. I brusquely said no, saying
this was not a theatrical performance with memorized dialogue. He
remained perfectly calm; he wanted only to know whether I was
going to stand by my deposition in the preliminary investigation. Of
course, I said, I told you the truth and will not tell the court
anything different. Would I admit to guilt? Certainly not. That
was the end of this conversation, which I mistakenly hoped would
be the last with this fellow.

Then came the hour of truth. We were led into the courtroom.
Here I saw Janka again, also for the first time since our court
confrontation in the spring. We solemnly looked into each other's
eyes. He said a long, dark tunnel was coming. And I in my
irrepressible optimism: Yes, but there is light at the end of it.

The courtroom was filled to the last seat. I recognized Anna,
Helene, Willi Bredel, and other writers. It seemed to me that they
nodded encouragingly to me. The rest were strangers, most of them
buried in the morning papers, people ordered there from factories
and state offices. Next to me sat: Janka, Zöger, and Richard Wolf.
The latter I had until then never met, although we allegedly
belonged to one and the same subversive circle: he was a program
director for the radio who had somehow come into contact with
Harich. In front of us the defense attorneys: Dr. Friedrich Wolff
for Janka and Wolf, Frau Dr. Schindowski for Zöger and me.

The court was presided over by the vice-president of the High
Court, Ziegler. One of the assessors was Judge Löwenthal, whom I
knew personally from a vacation in Ahrenshoop, where we had lived
under the same roof. The prosecution was represented by
Melsheimer and Jahnke. To the side sat a fat woman with a weird
hair style, like that worn by Frau Scholtz-Klink, leader of the Nazi
women's organization. That was Justice Minister Benjamin, who I
later learned was called "Red Hilda" by the prisoners. She
followed the trial with either a grimly severe or a smirking face.

During the formalities, recording of personal data, etc., there was
an omission worthy of note: the accused is customarily asked

whether he has seen the indictment and pleads guilty. We waited in vain for the second question. They wanted to spare themselves the embarrassment of having the defendants in such a large-scale show trial declare their innocence at the very beginning of the proceedings.

The charges, now presented alternately by Melsheimer and Jahnke, accused us of such weighty crimes against the state that the verdict, supposing the prosecutors believed in it themselves, could only have read "life." The trick was very simple: thoughts were translated into intentions, intentions into plans, everything ratcheted up by several degrees. The motives behind our ideas, our concepts for reform went completely unnoticed. Accordingly: We aspired to the unification of Germany, ergo we wanted to eradicate the GDR. We advocated reforms in agricultural policy, ergo we wanted to destroy socialist agriculture. We talked about who in the Party leadership could initiate such policies of reform, ergo we wanted to overthrow the Party leadership, above all Ulbricht, and at the same time the government. We thought the FDJ should become an umbrella organization for various youth groups, ergo we wanted to destroy unity among the youth. Our idea for self-administered factories with workers' councils and elected directors (which was not even original—it was being discussed everywhere and had been practiced in Yugoslavia for years) was branded as an anarchist-syndicalist attempt to undermine the socialist basis of the economy. And so on—it was easy to take the individual points out of context, change their purpose and underlying intent into the opposite, and presto: there for all to see was your plot against the very foundations of the GDR. To make things worse, we had constituted a circle (without knowing it), which Melsheimer "proved," taking a page from the book of the bloody hangman Vyshinskii. There was a grotesque twist to the theme of conspiracy, of plotting. In connection with the 1956 meeting with Janka on the Day of Repentance, the concept of a "Red 20th of July" was even broached (I forget by whom). Indeed, was it our fault that the Stalinists permitted no open discussion? That exactly like us, hundreds of "groups" (i.e., circles of like-minded people), were discussing the 20th Party Congress with its attack on Stalinism? We would much rather have handled these problems openly and candidly in the press. There had been no shortage of faint-hearted attempts, in *Sonntag*, in *Wochenpost*, in *Eulenspiegel*. For those responsible, the consequences had not failed to materialize. Although our work in *Sonntag* was not brought up at the trial—we do have a free press!—I am convinced that what triggered the legal action against us was precisely the articles in *Sonntag*, which for months had been a great vexation to those in power, as I have described in my diary. At the time, many editors at other papers were fired, for example the talented journalist and loyal old Communist Rudi Wetzel, formerly a member of the Central Committee, later the trusty and popular editor in chief of *Wochenpost*, in whose founding he had been actively involved. Never again could he engage in activities commensurate to his abilities. His eightieth birthday in January 1989 was not even mentioned in the media.

After the examination of all of us, the witnesses had their turn. A completely senseless and superfluous step, but it was part of the performance. What could they testify to that we ourselves had not already testified to? It was left to Harich to quote, by virtue of his phenomenal memory, remarks we had perhaps made in passing during conversations; these now lent credence to the charges and took on an incriminating function before the court. In this sense Harich played a nefarious role, and the name "Harich Group," which the Western media in their naiveté adopted uncritically, is completely inappropriate.

A strange figure was cut by *Sonntag* editor Hensel, whom Zöger, as his closest colleague, had had summoned as a defense witness. Hensel stood before the judge and said nothing. He gave only his name, and refused to answer any other questions, as if he were deaf and dumb. The court was forced to dismiss him, without his having done what he was expected to.

My wife had signed up as a witness, so as to see me again and plead for my innocence. As the witnesses marched in to take their oaths, Heide looked only at me, whom she had not seen in half a year. (Later she told me she was surprised and pleased at my healthy complexion—o helpful sunlamp!) Our exchange of glances did not last long because Melsheimer barked at her, telling her she should face the court. Actually, she belonged in the dock as an accessory, just like Lotte Janka; both had participated in the Atonement Day party characterized as "conspiratorial." But apparently the Stalinists did not take their own lies that seriously; neither Heide nor Lotte was subjected to Party proceedings on account of it, which would have been at least the minimum. Heide concentrated so hard on answering the questions about the nature of that gathering that she made an amusing slip. Zöger had for unfathomable reasons declared that he could not remember any details from that evening because he had had too much to drink. To a question in this connection, Heide, failing to recognize the intent of the question, replied no, Zöger never drank because he had a bad stomach. Zöger took it in with a resigned smile. In the meantime he had probably realized that his tactic did not fit the nature of this show and mock trial.

To summarize, not a single witness—except Harich—incriminated us, although they all visibly had to struggle with the fear that they might be forced to exchange the position of witness for one of defendant. Could they not be arraigned as accessories at any time? They were co-workers at the Aufbau-Verlag, in whose Party section things were discussed openly and critically. Wolf Düwel, Fritz Voigt, Günter Schubert, Müller-Claud—I cannot speak badly of their behavior as witnesses. What they subsequently brought forward as self-criticism is quite a different matter. Melsheimer had no shortage of subliminal, intimidating threats. I felt particularly sorry for Paul Merker. In a secret trial he had been sentenced to an eight-year term for alleged involvement in the Noel Field affair; he had not been out of prison very long. Also called to the stand was Jochen Wenzel, who came to such a bad end later on. He held up very steadfastly, even courageously.

Unfortunately, I did not know the code of criminal procedure. It became clear to me only from observing Janka's approach (suggested to him by his first-rate lawyer, Friedrich Wolff) that I could question the witnesses. The formula went: "I request the High Court to ask the witness . . . " We made extensive use of it, especially with Harich, until it went too far for Melsheimer and he interrupted: "They are going to want to know which street corner Harich was standing on when he said this or that . . . "

The statement for the defense was begun by Dr. Wolff, who argued persuasively that all the crimes charged to his client had the character of simple internal Party affairs, perhaps factional squabbling or other anti-Party behavior; he had in no way violated existing laws, hence the only possible verdict was acquittal. My defense lawyer, Dr. Schindowski, could not avoid pleading along the same lines, yet in her faint-heartedness she could not get the word "acquittal" past her lips, instead merely quoting the relevant paragraphs. She made a weak impression, was clearly in over her head, did not help me at all, and did only what I instructed. I would never have chosen her as my defender. One conversation was enough to tell me that. She was visibly more frightened than I. The more than one thousand marks Heide had to pay her was money down the drain.

Dr. Wolff behaved very bravely. After all, he was a Party member, at that time president of the lawyers' association of Berlin. He knew what was going on and that he was locking horns with the ruling power. To my knowledge, it is the only case in the many Stalinist show trials in any country in which the defendants pleaded not guilty and the defense lawyers moved for acquittal. It is that much more disgraceful that none of the observers present, among them highly decorated members of the academy, passed this fact on to the outside world. It remained as good as unknown; even Western sources did not mention it.

It was not as though harsh sentences had not been demanded by the prosecution: Janka five years' penitentiary, Just three and a half, Wolf four, Zöger two and a half. The legal justification with which Melsheimer concluded his thundering final statement was revealing: "We invoke Article 6 of the Constitution." We were thus convicted on the basis of an article of the constitution that forbade incitement to assassination, to war, to race-baiting, and to boycotting.

Then we were allowed concluding remarks. Janka kept his brief; he expressed barely contained, justified anger. He rejected the charges in their entirety as unjustified, and emphasized that for him, as throughout his more than thirty years as a Party member, the only issue was the well-being of the Party and of socialism. I admitted, if I remember correctly, to certain thoughtless deeds, but likewise rejected the charges altogether. Zöger went the farthest in self-criticism—the whole process had evidently affected him so strongly that he could not hold back tears. It was astounding to me how soft and sensitive this seemingly hard, even fierce man was on the inside. In a break in the trial, during which we sat together in a large cell in the courthouse, we were served a thick pea soup full of sausage and bacon. Out of nervousness, Zöger could not even touch his food. I therefore polished off both his and mine, saying: "We won't be getting anything this good for a while . . ."

The court, of course, complied with the recommendations of the state's attorney. My sentence was increased to four years and Wolf's shortened by half a year accordingly. Apparently the sum total of years was set in advance.

The performance was over, the curtain fell, the audience went home, no applause was heard. I could not shake the impression that the main actors, the three judges, also felt uncomfortable. Apparently the presiding judge, Ziegler, had not played his role to the directors' satisfaction: he was subsequently transferred to the regional court in Frankfurt an der Oder. What later became of him, I do not know. I hope he lives a long time, so that he can answer for this, among his many crimes against justice. Judge Löwenthal died shortly thereafter. Of the third judge I know nothing at all. Melsheimer has been dead for a long time. Nobody troubles his head over him anymore. The Minister of Justice also died recently (well over eighty), a member of the Central Committee to her last breath.

The producers of this spectacle must have believed that the deterrent effect had not gone far enough, for they subsequently staged a series of similar trials in the regional capitals. They did not want to suffer the humiliation again of not having any paragraph of the penal code to invoke and having to resort to Article 6 of the constitution. Thus a supplementary law was hurriedly appended to the penal code, under which, among others, my good friend Erich Loest was convicted. Imagine: convicted on grounds of a clause which, at the time he committed his alleged "crime," did not even exist! And moreover, the sentences handed down were incomparably more barbarous than ours: seven and a half years for Erich, who in our trial would have come away with two years at the most. I need not enlarge on this any further, since Erich Loest wrote an outstanding book on this shameful deed by the Stalinists, naming names and giving addresses—*Durch die Erde ein Riss*—from which I, as far as my own imprisonment goes, could easily recite whole pages.

The verdict was thus spoken. We were brought back to the U-boat. Back into the cell in which I had spent half a year—it was cell number 7—, hovering between hope and depression. Now the uncertainty was past, and I was seized with despair. Four years of penitentiary, not just prison—who knew what was in store for me. Four years separated from my wife: how would she manage with the children? Would they let her keep working in television? Would someone support her? Four years of not seeing my children, now ten and seven. When I was released, they would be fourteen and eleven. They needed their father! And my own father, sick in a TB sanitarium, would I even see him again? And my mother, who had not yet got over the early death of my brother, how would she take this new sorrow? Four years away from my own apartment, which we had finally created out of nothing, we refugees. No walks in the country, no vacations by the sea, in the mountains. The dark tunnel of which Janka had spoken now opened up before me in all its horror. I felt very small and helpless in the face of it. And suddenly I was overcome by convulsive sobbing, bottomless despair. I felt expelled, degraded, beaten down. And what was it all for?

Then I pulled myself together. In me something sprang up, something that protected me during the following dark years from falling prey to such despair again; something that helped me survive the time in prison spiritually and intellectually undamaged, remain steadfast, not cave in: defiance. Angry defiance, which in any case, was part of my heritage from my peasant forefathers from the Riesengebirge. These people we were dealing with had not gained their power through their own efforts, but had received it as a gift from the Red Army; now they were robbing me and others of our freedom, in defiance of justice and the law. I would not give them the satisfaction and knuckle under, resign myself, and fall into despair. No, I would remain resolute, stand by my opinions and, perhaps the day would come when they could be expressed publicly. That is why, in the years that followed up to today, not a word has been heard from me in which I recanted one iota of what I believed in 1956 was the right course for socialism in the GDR.

Interlude on Magdalenenstrasse in Berlin-Lichtenberg

I had to surrender my civilian clothes and received lightweight gray fatigues. It was the warmest part of summer. I now thought I would have to serve my sentence in Brandenburg or Bautzen, but far from it. The Stasi did not let me out of its clutches that quickly. I remained at their mercy until the beginning of February 1958. What lay behind it, I can only surmise. They transported me—in handcuffs, of course—to another Stasi prison in Berlin, to, as I later learned from Heide, the Stasi complex on Magdalenenstrasse. The cell was tiny, 9 by 4 1/2 feet. Again the back part of the room was taken up by a wooden cot with a mattress. The empty space in front was just large enough for calisthenics done in place. By way of compensation, the cell was not underground. It was bright and relatively cheerful. A guard once addressed me as Janka, so I knew that we had all ended up there. I now received the *Berliner Zeitung* every day, and was allowed to keep the psychology books Heide had sent me while I was awaiting trial. So I was not bored. The main thing now for me was to pass the time, no matter how.

Then I had the great pleasure of Heide's being allowed to visit me for the first time. We saw each other in the presence of the interrogator. Only a handshake, no hug, no kisses, no conversation about the trial and prison conditions. So we spoke about the children, about Heide's work in television, which she was allowed to continue on the condition that the name Just not appear on the screen. She had been summoned before the Party leadership right after my arrest, where it had been strongly suggested to her that she acknowledge my guilt, and distance herself from me to some extent. She had refused, of course: Her husband was innocent, and one should wait for the verdict, if one ever came. I was never given a copy of the verdict, and neither was Heide; at the television station they never brought up the matter again.

I had just read in the newspaper that Molotov, Malenkov, and Kaganovich had been removed from the picture, and because I was clutching at every straw, I said out of deep conviction to Heide during the visit: If Molotov has been forced to go, others will have to go, too. I was naturally thinking of Ulbricht and his people, which Heide understood, while the interrogator watching us was evidently thinking of other opponents of Khrushchev's; otherwise he would have certainly picked up on this remark of mine. Again this was unforgivable naiveté, unfounded wishful thinking, as indeed during my entire four years of imprisonment I never gave up hope that I would soon be amnestied. Yet perhaps precisely this delusion made it easier or even possible to survive. If I had known the whole time that I would sit out all but three months of the four years—I am not sure such a clear realization would not have crushed me. At the same time it should have startled me, among other things, that in the room where Heide's visit took place, a huge portrait of the generalissimo in full dress uniform hung on the wall—more than a year after Khrushchev's denunciation of Stalin. Janka told me later that in the U-boat while on his way to see the doctor, he had seen a similar portrait of Stalin. The Stalinists never renounced their idol. They will always find rationalizations, even as more and more crimes of this tyrant are uncovered. They are useless when it comes to new thinking, to new policies. To remain in power, they will change their stripes, but in their hearts they will remain Stalin's heirs.

It soon became clear to me why the Stasi was keeping me in its custody. New interrogations began. This time it had to do not with me, but with friends and acquaintances in Leipzig. What did I know about Erich Loest and Jochen Wenzel? Nothing at all about Loest, and about Wenzel only that he was an editor at the *Börsenblatt* and also wrote for *Sonntag* on occasion. Zöger knew him from his days in Leipzig, and we had made an effort to recruit Wenzel for our newspaper—we considered him an extremely capable journalist. He informed us about happenings in Leipzig, above all the infamous smear campaign that Henniger, the regional secretary of the Cultural League there, was conducting against us, especially against me. I thus had in good conscience virtually nothing to say about Jochen Wenzel. It soon became clear to me where the questioning was leading. In Leipzig the case against Ralf Schröder, Erich Loest, and others was being prepared. Wenzel was also to be implicated. He was supposed to have served as the contact between the opposition in Leipzig and us, so that a country-wide conspiracy could be constructed. In any case, the interrogator did not hesitate to drop threatening hints that our case might be reopened in a larger context. Why it never came to that, I do not know. Evidently the death of Jochen Wenzel had something to do with it. Although ill with cancer of the liver, he was not released, but had to spend the last months of his young life in a prison hospital.

The trials in Halle and elsewhere took place as scripted. Much harsher sentences than ours were imposed on the defendants, although there was much less with which to work. After all, Harich had established connections to the West that could be characterized as unlawful, if one insisted, and we had published many critical pieces in *Sonntag*, which could easily provoke those in power—although it never should and could have led to a conviction in court. Those in power realized, however, that one could not swing Article 6 like a club if one did not want to discredit the whole constitution. Thus the newly-enacted addendum contained articles pertaining to treason against the state, and activity hostile or subversive to the state, and much harsher penalties were established for individual violations. A relic of the Stalin Era and the Cold War as indefensible as the further addendum enacted after the Biermann Affair. Shame and dishonor on the deputies of the People's Chamber who raised their hands to vote for such inhumane laws that violate fundamental human rights.

The time in the prison on Magdalenenstrasse passed more quickly, although it lasted just as long as pre-trial detention. I read a lot, studied books on psychology, also was sent literary works and drafted poems and stories in my head. I learned how to communicate with the cell next to mine by means of tapping on the walls. One tap for A, two for B and so on, after every word two short taps, whereupon the person in the next cell would do the same to show he had understood. When it grew quiet in the building after the evening headcount, we would begin our conversation. My neighbor was a soldier convicted of desertion—if he was telling the truth. I kneaded tiny chess figures out of bread, with which I played on an imaginary board.

After the depressing Easter holiday in pre-trial detention, the first Christmas behind bars proved tolerable. On 5 February I was hauled out of my cell, still in the thin overalls they had issued me in the summer. I was then loaded—in handcuffs, of course—into a prison van divided into tiny cells by thin metal partitions. I could barely sit, even motionless, with my shackled hands on my knees. That I survived this long trip in my thin overalls in February cold without substantial damage to my health is due only to the rage that burned in me at this cruel, inhumane form of transportation, and kept my blood warm. We stopped once on the way. I heard women's voices; one or more female prisoners were unloaded. It was already dark when we reached our destination. I say "we" because I learned later on that Janka, Zöger, and Wolf were sitting in the same "black Maria" and shivering from the cold. On the outside it was disguised as a baker's delivery van. We were hauled out one by one and led to our cells. We had ended up at Bautzen II (Mättigstrasse), which was to be our penitentiary in the coming years.

From the newspaper I later learned that on the day before our transfer to the penitentiary, a CC meeting had taken place at which Schirdewan and Wollweber were expelled from the CC. Among other things, they were charged with having wanted to hinder the struggle against counterrevolutionary groups. That could have only meant us, and I suspect that these two at least expressed opposition to the scandalous trials. That might be the second reason why the Stasi kept us in custody for half a year after the verdict was pronounced. Apparently the final word had not been spoken—after all, Wollweber was the minister for state security.

It is regrettable that Schirdewan himself said not one word about this period during a private conversation with Janka, with whom he had operated in the same anti-fascist resistance group; he could have shed more light on the mysterious and intricate state of affairs for us as well as for historians. He will take it to his grave like so many others (Oelssner, Grotewohl, Fechner, Merker, Herrnstadt, Zaisser, Ziller, Selbmann, Apelt), without having given his view of things to future generations. History is always written by the victors, after all. Yet revision of the "victors'" account by the defeated would be an invaluable source of insight for avoiding errors and wrong directions in the future. What did Bukharin and his comrades really want? Will we ever learn the truth, the whole truth? *Perestroika* and *glasnost* hold out hope.

Bautzen II

Erich Loest has given an impressive and authentic account of conditions in this "special slammer" in his book *Durch die Erde ein Riss*. The three years I spent there would yield enough material for a thick book—if I had the ability and the desire to write it. Space limitations force me to restrict myself to certain facts that prove that what we experienced there had nothing to do with modern, humane criminal justice. It is ironic that in the Weimar Republic the Communists, in alliance with leftist intellectuals, were pioneers in the struggle for penal reform. Yet once they came to power, they introduced practices that defy description. When I hear of terrorists imprisoned in the Federal Republic complaining about their "solitary confinement," it makes me smile. I sat for over two years in strictest solitary confinement, including during pre-trial detention. That meant: alone in my cell, alone during exercise in the yard, work likewise alone in the cell. During this time I saw no one except the guards, and could not talk to anyone, because there was, of course, no talking to the guards.

The cells were furnished minimally: one small table bolted to the wall, likewise a bench, a narrow folding bed, a tiny shelf on the wall, in the corner a toilet bowl and a stool, that was all. The walls were painted in dark gray enamel up to eye-level, on the ceiling a lightbulb in a small metal cage. The barred window offered a view of the roof of the institution, in which, as I later learned, a court and pre-trial detention facility were also housed. One was not allowed to lie down during the day, so I walked back and forth for hours: seven steps in one direction, seven steps in the other. Deep-breathing exercises under the window, knee-bends, push-ups, so as not to go slack.

At first there was no work, for it was a privilege one had to earn. After several weeks, a box full of Bakelite spoons was brought to my cell, along with emery paper, ribbons, and pieces of cellophane. The egg spoons had been made in a mold and had sharp, uneven front and back edges that had to be sanded down. Six spoons in different colors had to be tied together with a ribbon and wrapped in cellophane. (I wonder whether the purchasers of such spoons ever suspect where they are packaged?) I gave it a lot of effort, and the spoons I prepared during the first three days certainly caused their later users no trouble. On the third day the guard demanded that I fulfill my quota. Up to then I had produced seventy to eighty such packets of spoons a day. The quota was seven hundred! I thought that must be impossible, but the guard brusquely informed me that the others were achieving the quota and, if I didn't, I would not be allowed to buy anything. Fine, I thought, let people cut their mouths on the spoons, and so I gave each spoon a lick and a promise with the emery paper, and I made my quota.

Later I had to press snap-fasteners into perforated cards, work that soon gave me sore fingertips. The following work was the most pleasant: there were switches that had to be wired. The wires had to be cut to size beforehand and bent with a special tool, the ends isolated. At the end I had to work on the baseplates and coverplates for cameras. They had been stamped in a press and now had to be finished with clean edges. What I earned by the hour was never revealed to me. Most of my earnings were withheld for "room and board." For my personal use I received five to ten marks a month, with which I could buy margarine, wurst, and things like that. Luckily I am not a smoker; the smokers spent most of their money on cigarettes.

I was not allowed to say my name to anyone. I was only "Prisoner Number 4/58." The door would be opened, I had to stand at attention and report: "Cell 4, occupied by one prisoner, Prisoner 4 slash 58 reporting." When leaving for my recreation I had to announce my departure and then my return. I had to salute every guard I met and report in the same way. The degrading regulations of a Prussian-style militaristic penal system combined with the evil practices of the Soviet system, a truly loathsome synthesis. Recreation, exercise in the yard, lasted no longer than twenty, at most thirty minutes. One walked alone in a circle, and had to do prescribed calisthenics at sixteen different speeds. Above the walls that divided the small individual courtyards a guard glared down from a cage. One time he snapped at the prisoner in the courtyard next to mine that he should do the exercises correctly. The prisoner, whose voice I recognized as Harich's, apologized obsequiously, saying he could not do the exercises any other way. "Do them like the guy in the yard next to you," commanded the sentry, whom I promptly dubbed the Wall-Watcher.

The day began at five a.m. with a loud bell that woke us up. Then came morning headcount and breakfast. After six o'clock was work in the cell. At twelve there was lunch, at six o'clock dinner, at seven o'clock the evening headcount and lockup. After this you were allowed to lie down. In the evening you had to undress down to your undershirt and underwear. Your things, including the tin bowl and cap, then had to be arranged neatly on the stool and placed outside the door. Even glasses had to be handed over. In the morning you got your things back. In the cell you were allowed to sit in pants and a shirt, when it was cold in a woolen vest; you wore old smelly leather slippers on your feet. For exercise in the yard you had to put on a jacket, along with high-topped boots without the laces, on your head a kind of beret, which had to be tipped to every guard, while you looked him in the eyes, of course.

Once every week or two you could order a book, which at my normal reading pace I had to read several times to keep myself occupied. You could request that a chess set be brought to your cell. I spent hours over the chessboard. I alternately let white, then black win. Movie showings were also offered on occasion. As a prisoner in solitary confinement, I would be brought into the darkened theater where the prisoners in group confinement had already been seated. We prisoners from solitary were placed at long intervals, one to a row.

One time the guard who led me in made a mistake: he left before I had sat down. I spied Erich Loest two rows ahead of me and in a flash moved next to him. We talked quietly during the entire film, of which I took in nothing—it was "A Human Destiny" by Bondartschuk. Erich was only a few cells away from me, and I had heard his voice before when he reported in from his walk in the yard. The encounter in the theater remained our only meeting, alas. We would have had a lot to talk about.

Once I also ran into Ralf Schröder in a peculiar fashion. I did not know him personally, having only read of his case in the newspaper. When my strict solitary confinement was lifted and I was walking around in the yard with a group of other prisoners, someone was behind me, who, in defiance of regulations, had taken off his hat in the warm sun and opened the top button of his uniform jacket. It was not long before the guard reprimanded him severely. Quietly, so that no one else heard, I asked him who he was. He countered like an experienced "slammerologist," asking who I was. I told him my name, with which he was apparently so familiar that his jaw dropped in surprise. Then he told me his name. With him, too, I unfortunately had no further contact. (I understand why the prisoners from the Red Army Faction want and demand to be put together; a conversation with like-minded people can brighten even the grimmest imprisonment.)

Due to an oversight by the guards I also managed to have a conversation with Kurt Vieweg in the showers, to which we were taken on the weekend. We knew each other from before. When I was secretary of the Quedlinburg district administration I had had to settle a quarrel with sectarian comrades who refused to accept our policy of cooperating with the bourgeois scholars Prof. Hans Stubbe and Prof. Becker. Then Vieweg, at the time secretary of the CC for agriculture, came to my assistance. And after 17 June, 1953, we were involved in agitation together, he as a member and I as staff of the CC, at a plant in the Adlershof area that had gone on strike. Now he was in Bautzen for eight years. He had, as a member of the technical staff of the Academy for Agricultural Sciences, developed an outline of agricultural policy very similar to ours. Ideas for reform were in the air. After our arrest he had become fearful and fled to the West. On Ulbricht's orders, an old friend, the editor in chief of *BZ am Abend*, Ernst Hantsch (if my memory serves me right), persuaded him to return, saying nothing would happen to him. Once back, he was immediately arrested and convicted in a secret trial. He hurriedly told me all this with great bitterness while we stood in the showers. I never saw him again.

The same was true of Georg Dertinger, the former minister for foreign affairs of the GDR. During the time I had to assemble the switches, I had to go around at the end of the workday accompanied by the work brigade leader, also a prisoner, and collect the finished pieces from the individual cells and bring them to the freight elevator. Dertinger brought finished pieces from another cellblock. Every day we were able hastily to exchange a few sentences by the elevator. This went on for weeks, so that a genuine conversation with very long gaps resulted. From him I learned that, on orders from the Soviets and Grotewohl, he had negotiated with the Americans about their conditions for reunification. The Americans' first demand was that an independent SPD be allowed in the GDR. On these or other grounds the Soviets lost interest in the talks. And Dertinger was held responsible. Thus his description of it, for whose veracity I admittedly cannot vouch. If only I had visited him after he was amnestied, as I intended—but he took it to the grave. Will his descendants and friends see to it that the truth about this case, about this prisoner, also comes to light?

Contact with one's relatives was kept to a minimum. Once a month I was allowed to write a letter of twenty lines, mentioning nothing about my "crime," nothing about "prison conditions." And was allowed to receive the same kind of letter. Later on both my children were allowed to add greetings. And once every three months my wife was allowed to visit me for half an hour. Beforehand I would be shaved and put in a new uniform. In the presence of the director or one of his deputies we were allowed to converse, only about private matters. Only a handshake, no kisses, no hug. I will confine myself to these bare facts; throughout history enough has already been written about the feelings of prisoners under such conditions.

For my birthday I was allowed, assuming good behavior, to receive a package, which Heide packed with all her love and care. Among other things, fruit was allowed to be sent, and one time she thought of raisins. These were confiscated; raisins were not fruit. The fact that they came from grapes was too difficult for the gentlemen to grasp. Unfortunately my birthday fell in June, so that the sausage Heide sent had to be eaten quickly, much too quickly. For Christmas I was not allowed to receive a package, but had to send one home. Such a perversion had never before been thought of by a German prison administration. At first I refused, of course, whereupon they blackmailed me—if I did not comply, I would not be allowed to buy anything, and I knuckled under. Thus my wife, who celebrated Christmas with the children at her parents', received a package there from the penitentiary; it contained pralines, fountain pens, sweets, and other things I had chosen from a list. The package brought joy to no one, on the contrary.

Meals were adequate: I did not starve or suffer any symptoms of deficiencies—except for kidney stones, which built up as a result of a lack of fluids and had to be removed after my release from prison; the operation almost cost me my life. We were given enough bread. Lunch usually consisted of stew. Every so often there were potatoes boiled in their skins, along with herring or a boiled egg, now and then meatballs on Sundays. For supper we were given on some days twenty-five grams of margarine or lard, on other days fifty grams of sausage. Both had to last for two days. For breakfast there was gruel and toast and jam. As a beverage, watery malt coffee, occasionally tea. On the tenth anniversary of the GDR, which, despite all our hopes, passed without the greatly longed-for amnesty, the smell of real coffee suddenly wafted throughout the prison. "The pigs are guzzling real coffee," my cellmate cursed, "and we get dishwater." He was mistaken. On this day even we prisoners received real coffee and a piece of cake, the only time. A list of everything I was deprived of for four years would be interesting: rolls, grilled meat, beer, seltzer, soda, tropical fruits, cocoa, chocolate, to name only a few. But as one can see, a person can live without such delicacies.

On the day before Christmas 1958—I had almost two years of strictest solitary confinement behind me—a bed was set up in my cell, and soon a prisoner appeared, with his possessions wrapped in a blanket. "My name is Benno Szuminski, I'm Polish, in for life, was the Frogman, maybe you've heard of me, and who are you?" Yes, I remembered a trial before the High Court against an American spy who had been intercepted on his way to Poland. He had a wet suit with him because he was supposed to swim across the Oder River. So that was Benno, my cellmate for a year and a half, a member of the Home Army during the war, who went underground after the war to escape persecution, a partisan for years against the new authorities in Poland and the Soviets, then fled to the West, where he was pressured by the Americans into signing on as an agent. Politically we were worlds apart, but we understood each other on a human basis—what choice did we have? I learned Polish songs from Benno. He noticed that the long period of solitary confinement had been very hard on me, and entertained me daily with stories and funny anecdotes from his life. I am indebted to him for my deep personal affection for the Polish people, a partiality I will always keep. When we got into arguments, he cursed me as a red fascist and I him as a white fascist. As I later learned from Erich Loest, Benno was known and loved throughout the entire penitentiary because he had made an escape attempt. He was later amnestied, and reportedly emigrated to America, where he died. Several months before my release we were separated, so that my more than two years of solitary confinement were rounded out.

I will never forget this fine companion who shared a cell with me for months during the most difficult period of my life. I will never forget how in the evening, when sausages were handed out, he would make a beeline for them, so that with an eagle eye he could grab—the smaller one(!). I would protest in vain—You need it more than I do, was his standard response. On the other hand I will also not forget—nor did he, as long as he lived—, how once, during exercise in the yard, I noticed a cigarette butt on the ground, a treasure for Benno, who was a heavy smoker; I immediately put it in my pocket. In the cell it proved to be not a cigarette butt, but rather jackdaw droppings, colored white and brown, virtually identical to the coveted left-over.

That the penal administration was not pursuing humanitarian goals by giving me this cellmate was clear—a dissident Communist put in with an American spy who hated the Soviets, who despised people's democracy, a dedicated follower of Pilsudski. Janka likewise was given a spy from a Western secret service as his cellmate. It did not work, though: we left politics aside and got along wonderfully on a human level.

From time to time I was summoned to the director, where in the presence of a civilian, a Stasi agent called "Uncle" by the prisoners, a "heart check-up" was conducted. How did I now feel about my crime—they wanted to hear acknowledgment and remorse. I was never ready to oblige. My standard answer to this first question was: "I am still unaware that I have committed a crime, and feel I was unjustly convicted." For this reason the conversation always ended very quickly. They were somewhat satisfied when, after a long time in prison, I admitted that I had never been a true communist, but always a social democrat. They were the true communists, how could there be other, possibly even better ones! And in actuality—the reform-minded communists of then and now, to use this oversimplifying term for once, are closer to the social democrats (the ones on the left, it goes without saying) than to their communist comrades, who actually felt right at home under Stalin.

Was the time I had to spend in Bautzen II totally wasted? I had so much time, and how gladly would I have used it constructively. I thus asked to be allowed to do translation, because I had made up my mind that after my release, I would try to get into a job using my knowledge of Czech, perhaps even make a career of it. In a conversation with the institute director and "Uncle" this wish of mine was refused. When I pointed out that Rosa Luxemburg wrote during her imprisonment and was allowed to translate Korolenko, and that was under the Kaiser, they answered: "We're no longer under the Kaiser!" How true! These people were of course unaware of the telling irony of their comment, they who considered themselves communists, members of what, according to their claim, was the most progressive movement now in existence.

With that I can conclude my memories of the period of awakening that followed the 20th Party Congress of the CPSU, of my activities with *Sonntag*, of the passionate discussions among socialists ready and willing to carry out reform, and their persecution by the Stalinists. These memories should make it plain that we were working in the direction today characterized by the concepts *perestroika*, *glasnost*, and new thinking. Since the war the international communist movement has had three major opportunities to break out of inflexibility and a lack of perspective, and set out for new shores: 1956—20th Party Congress, de-Stalinization, radical transformation in Poland. 1968—Prague Spring, Dubcek's solution of socialism with a human face. Both opportunities were destroyed by incorrigible, reactionary conservatives. Today, in the late eighties, the third chance— Gorbachev's *perestroika*, *glasnost*, new thinking. There will not be a fourth opportunity. Either these policies will be implemented throughout the whole communist movement, or the entire thing will go down as an episode in the history of socialism. Because in the GDR practically the same people are in power who eagerly helped to destroy the previous two opportunities—during which they went so far as to let their army join the march on Czechoslovakia, an unprecedented example of a short-sighted display of power, far removed from any ideal of a humanitarian, democratic socialism—one cannot be surprised that in defiance of all reality, they cling to their rigid position, remaining frozen in the past. As I write these lines, in mid-September 1989, thousands of young GDR citizens are voting with their feet, using Hungary as a transit-point to Austria and the Federal Republic. And thousands are applying for legal travel visas, so that the number of people going to the Federal Republic this year will reach 100,000 or even more. All warnings to these leaders, from whatever source, are futile—they must go. The big question is only where the new leaders are supposed to come from and how they are going to get us out of this rut. At present I have no answer to this question, and I do not know anyone who does. Time will tell whether socialist ideals can remain strong enough in Germany to win over a majority of the people.

—Prenden, summer of 1989

Communist Jargon

In Communist East German usage, certain words and phrases carried specific political connotations. As in other Communist countries, the jargon was developed to make language (like other forms of culture) serve ideological ends. The following list is provided to alert the reader to terms in *Witness in His Own Cause* that should be recognized as politically weighted.*

Agitation (*Agitation*)
Anarchism (*Anarchismus*)
Bureaucratism (*Bürokratismus*)
Careerism (*Karrierismus*)
Censor (*Zensor*)
Comrade (*Genosse*)
Conciliator (*Versöhnler*)
Conscious (*Bewusst*)
Counterrevolution(ary)
(*Konterrevolution(är)*)
Criticism and self-criticism
(*Kritik und Selbstkritik*)
Cult of personality
(*Personenkult*)
Dogmatism (*Dogmatismus*)
Faction (*Faktion*)
Formalism (*Formalismus*)

Inciting to boycott
(*Boykotthetze*)
Intervention (*Intervention*)
Liquidation (*Liquidierung*)
Masses (*Massen*)
People's democracy
(*Volksdemokratie*)
Policy of cooperation
(*Bündnispolitik*)
Race-baiting (*Rassenhetze*)
Region (*Bezirk*)
Restoration (*Restauration*)
Spontaneity (*Spontaneität*)
Syndicalism (*Syndikalismus*)
Terror (*Terror*)
Transmission belt
(*Transmissionsriemen*)
Warmongering (*Kriegshetze*)

---

*For detailed explications of these terms, see:

Gérard Bekerman, *Marx and Engels: A Conceptual Concordance* (Oxford: Basil Blackwell, 1983).
R.N. Carew Hunt, *A Guide to Communist Jargon* (New York: Macmillan, 1957).
Lester De Koster, *Vocabulary of Communism* (Grand Rapids, Michigan: William B. Eerdmans, 1964).
Hans R. Reich, *Sprache und Politik: Münchener Germanistische Beiträge* (Munich: Max Hueber, 1968), vol. 1.

Index

About the Author

Gustav Just was born on 16 June 1921 in Gablonz, a town in the German-speaking area of northern Bohemia (now in the Czech Republic). The son of a working-class father, he completed university-preparatory school and then volunteered for the army, ending the war as a lieutenant. When Germans were forced out of his homeland in 1946, he settled in Quedlinburg, where he worked as a teacher, and then, after a bout with tuberculosis, for the SED. He rose to become First Secretary of the German Writers' Union and then editor in chief of the intellectual journal *Sonntag*. He was sentenced to four years' imprisonment in 1957, accused of plotting to overthrow the state. After his release, he began working as a freelance translator of Czech and Slovak literature, eventually translating over one hundred books and plays. When the GDR crumbled in 1989, Just was instrumental in reestablishing the Social Democratic Party in the province of Brandenburg, where he was elected to the state parliament as its oldest member. He played an active role as a respected political figure until his withdrawal from public life in mid-March 1992, and now lives in retirement in Prenden.